GODDESS: THE CLASSICAL MODE

GODDESS: THE CLASSICAL MODE

Harold Koda

The Metropolitan Museum of Art
Yale University Press, New Haven and London

This volume has been published in conjunction with
the exhibition "Goddess," held at The Metropolitan Museum of Art
from May 1, 2003, through August 3, 2003.

The exhibition is made possible by

GUCCI

Additional support has been provided by

CONDÉ NAST
PUBLICATIONS

Published by The Metropolitan Museum of Art, New York

John P. O'Neill, Editor in Chief

Gwen Roginsky, Associate General Manager of Publications

Barbara Cavaliere, Editor

Design by Takaaki Matsumoto, Matsumoto Incorporated, New York

Elisa Frohlich, Production Manager

Cataloging-in-Publication data is available from the Library of Congress.

ISBN: 0-58839-047-0 (hc; The Metropolitan Museum of Art)

ISBN: 0-58839-048-9 (pbk; The Metropolitan Museum of Art)

ISBN: 0-300-09882-0 (Yale University Press)

Color separations by Professional Graphics Inc., Rockford, Illinois

Printed by Brizzolis Arte en Gráficas, Madrid

Bound by Encuadernación Ramos, S.A., Madrid

Printing and binding coordinated by Ediciones El Viso, S.A., Madrid

Unless otherwise indicated, the costume photography in this volume is by
Karin L. Willis, The Photograph Studio, The Metropolitan Museum of Art.

Cover: Madeleine Vionnet, French (1876–1975). Evening pajamas of white
silk crepe with matching scarves, 1931. Photograph: George
Hoyningen-Huene / Vogue © Condé Nast Publications Inc.

Frontispiece: Roman copy of Greek original. *Dancing Maenad (follower of the
god Dionysos)*, marble relief, ca. 27 B.C.–14 A.D. The Metropolitan Museum
of Art, Fletcher Fund, 1935 (35.11.3). Photograph: Scott Houston

Contents

6

SPONSOR'S STATEMENT

8

FOREWORD BY PHILIPPE DE MONTEBELLO

10

INTRODUCTION

20

PANDORA'S BOX: THE CHITON, PEPLOS, AND HIMATION

88

THE METAMORPHOSES: CLASSICAL TRANSFORMATIONS
AND CONTEMPORARY PERMUTATIONS

132

PYGMALION'S GALATEA: ART TO LIFE

178

MYTHIC DETAILS: THE GREEK KEY, LAURELS,
AND THE ATTRIBUTES OF GODDESSES

218

DEFINITIONS

220

SELECTED BIBLIOGRAPHY

221

ACKNOWLEDGMENTS

SPONSOR'S STATEMENT

I've always believed it is the privilege and the responsibility of a design company to encourage artistic expression of all kinds. As a fashion designer, I find it particularly meaningful to support The Metropolitan Museum of Art's Costume Institute. The Costume Institute is one of the most influential cultural institutions in the fashion world, and its exhibitions, with their extraordinary collection of artifacts and profound understanding of style and design, are legend. This collaboration between The Metropolitan Museum of Art and Gucci is deeply gratifying, because it brings two centuries of fashion, art, and design to a large and varied popular audience.

"Goddess" is a celebration of women, of fashion, and of the beauty of the human form. The title says it all. By exploring the enduring myths and iconic power of classical dress—an aesthetic that has inspired every fashion designer that has ever lived—"Goddess" also explores fashion's essential question: What rare combination of fortitude and grace makes women, and the clothes that adorn them, objects of worship?

Supporting The Costume Institute is a great source of pride for Gucci, and "Goddess" is a very significant addition to our legacy of sponsorship of the arts.

Tom Ford

FOREWORD

Conceived and carried to fruition by Harold Koda, Curator in Charge of The Costume Institute, The Metropolitan Museum of Art, "Goddess" is the newest of a suite of exhibitions that link The Costume Institute's extraordinary holdings with the collections of the Metropolitan's other curatorial departments. Costume, of course, appears in our galleries, in a variety of mediums and across diverse periods and cultures. Last year, "Extreme Beauty: The Body Transformed" included works from the departments Arts of Africa, Oceania, and the Americas; Arms and Armor; Prints and Drawings; European Paintings; Asian Art; and European Sculpture and Decorative Arts to substantiate its premise of the mutable nature of feminine beauty. Now, "Goddess" argues the reverse, that in costume and the arts, elements of classical dress have persisted as an ideal for over two-and-a-half millennia.

The works that appear in this book and the exhibition it accompanies focus primarily on the invigorated classicism of the twentieth century. Designs from the earlier part of the century are mostly from the remarkable holdings of The Costume Institute, with important examples from private collectors, many of whom are old friends of the department and the Museum. In addition, the more recent examples have been secured from the archives of designers and design houses. Although they were approached for loans for the exhibition, in many notable instances, the designers have offered their works as gifts to the Museum. This generosity has both enhanced the publication and the exhibition and expanded the breadth and encyclopedic nature of our permanent collection.

On behalf of the Museum, it is my sincere pleasure to acknowledge Gucci's outstanding support of the exhibition and its accompanying catalogue. Our heartfelt gratitude is also extended to Condé Nast for its exceptional commitment to this project. Culture and ideas survive through art. "Goddess" reaches back to ancient Greek times to continue The Costume Institute's ongoing commitment to extend this knowledge through fashion and encourage future scholarship.

"Goddess" suggests the abiding resonance of classical forms through the medium of dress. This aesthetic strand also stitches together the various arts at the Museum. Like the thread of Ariadne, the unbroken line of classical influence winds through the Metropolitan Museum's galleries.

Philippe de Montebello
Director
The Metropolitan Museum of Art

INTRODUCTION

Whether manifested as embracing revival or as smug repudiation, fashion is especially explicit in its address of history. While no era is without a consciousness of the past, the decades since 1980 have been particularly rich in the variety of strategies that fashion designers have employed to infuse their work with historical narratives. Initially, much of the referencing had the skin-deep, boldly graphic quality of a Michael Graves façade–immediately recognizable with familiar allusions, ironic and knowing playfulness, and unapologetic and unflinching superficiality.

Over the years, with the influence of certain Japanese designers, most consistently Rei Kawakubo of Comme des Garçons, and a new generation of Belgians, the Antwerp Six, a conceptually transgressive methodology emerged. For these designers, history is tumbled and assimilated. Unlike the bright juxtaposition of old forms-newly minted that is visible in architectural postmodernism, the new historicism finds expression in elements that have eroded and melded into ambiguous morphologies. Like the works of deconstructivist architect Peter Eisemann, these designers seem to highlight the unstable junctures and tensions of contradictory narratives. Theirs is a train wreck of history, with periods no longer discrete but piled, twisted, and welded into new forms, in which the focus shifts to the tenuous balance created by collapse rather

than by the lucidity of linear alignment.

Although fashion is predicated on a rather accelerated cycle of innovation and obsolescence, there have been numerous instances of its impulse to forms of immutable ideal beauty. Invariably, the invocation of designs impervious to the capriciousness of fashion has resulted in a referencing of the Hellenic antique. Like the mythic attributes of Græco-Roman gods and goddesses, discrete classicizing motifs and conventions have been, and continue to be, the mechanism by which ephemeral fashions are imbued with an ostensible sense of timeless and enduring beauty. Some of the elements establishing a transcendent association with the antique directly cite the costume types observed through ancient artworks, whether sculpture, wall frescoes, or red-and-black figure vase paintings. For example, the caryatids on the Acropolis in Athens which support the south porch of the Erechtheum, as seen above, have conveyed, since the fifth century B.C., the details of the peplos, the most characteristically Greek of ancient garments.

Often, the semiotic elements that transform contemporaneous fashion into a classical style are derived not from the somewhat scant evidence of the realities of classical dress but from representational effects seen in sculpture and painting. That is, details in line or stone that are an

Greek, attributed to Alkamenes (student of Pheidias). *Temple of the Caryatids, Erechtheum*, ca. 420 B.C. Photograph: Scala/Art Resource, NY

artistic elaboration on actual dress are reinterpreted again in cloth. This transition from apparel to art and from art back to apparel results in an exaggeration of the qualities of cloth, drapery, even garment construction that might or might not have existed in the original examples.

While the art of classical Greece was distinguished by its apparent impulse to an idealized naturalism, artistic stylizations and conventions inevitably intruded. Even the canon of proportion epitomized in the work of the Greek sculptor Polyclitus suggests that the intention of artists was not so much to describe their world as to perfect upon it. When it is represented in art, costume is another device for the propelling of narrative, the underscoring of character or role, and the introduction of formal elements that are purely compositional. In many instances, drapery is used both as structural support of the marble figure (often a copy of a bronze original), and to accentuate movement, like the Nike sneaker "swoosh" logo or the lines animating the gesture of a cartoon figure. The ability of drapery to suggest animation has been taken from classical art and applied to contemporary design.

Sometimes, the references are limited to individual details taken from ancient dress styles. But these are reconfigured to conform to prevailing contemporary aesthetics, often in deviation from

and sometimes in opposition to actual historical precedents. The stylized rendering of fluted folds of the fifth-century B.C. bronze statue the *Charioteer of Delphi*, for example, seen in the illustration above, provided the inspiration for the tightly pleated gowns of the Spanish-born painter and designer Mariano Fortuny, examples of whose work are shown on pages 174–175. Another frequent and perhaps more facile conjuring of the antique is simply the overlay of decorative elements such as key and wave meander patterns associated with Græco-Roman art and architecture onto conventionally fashionable contemporary styles.

From the Renaissance on, artists have attempted to dress their classical subjects in reasonable approximations of historical dress. In turn, designers have referenced the costumes depicted in these artworks, absorbing the inventive aspects of these later interpretive reconstructions with the same avidity that drives their citation of historical models. Most designers would never purport to aspire to an academic understanding of the classical forms they quote. Even those with a deeper interest in the meanings and contexts of their references are necessarily encumbered by the difficulty of determining the authenticity of classical dress. While it would appear that the most popular transmitter of Hellenic dress would be the artworks from the Græco-Roman period, it is as likely that later interpretations of antique modes have been and continue to be the sources for classical revivals.

Despite the increasing interest in and knowledge of the antique that occurred by the eighteenth century, the antiquarian impulse in artistic representation was limited to painters of grand subjects. Portrait painters who dressed their aristocratic sitters as nymphs, muses, or goddesses were often less attentive to historical fact, although they acknowledge as Bernard Rudofsky did in his book *Are Clothes Modern?* that: "Since all dressmakers' fashions carry the germ of future ridicule in them, the painter and sculptor take refuge in sartorial anachronisms." Those historical styles were often of the classical antique, and depicted a schematized version of a typically fashionable period gown. The suggestion of classical precedents appeared only in the gown's seamless and achromatic rendering, in the disarray of the chemise or underdress, in a disengaged shoulder strap, or more explicitly in the catching up of a turbulent volume of cloth with a diagonal harness. It was not until the second half of the eighteenth century that the introduction of an uncorseted, unpanniered, and therefore more cylindrical silhouette for the representation of classical dress, a popular classicizing convention already established in history painting, was

embraced by portrait painters. The well-known depiction by Angelica Kaufmann of Louis XVI's queen, Marie Antoinette, in a white cotton gown *à la chemise* was not in neoclassical taste. It did, however, anticipate in fashion and confirm as suitable for portraiture a style of dress at radical odds with the firmly corseted and voluminous silhouettes of formal eighteenth-century dress.

By the late eighteenth century, the interest in the Græco-Roman past was manifest in all areas of art and design. Despite the heightened antiquarian interest and desire for scholarly rigor, the actual dress styles of the period were evocations rather than literal citations of ancient forms. Although, in 1794, the painter Jacques Louis David was charged by the Société Républicaine et Populaire des Arts to costume the new republican age, his submission of designs with distinct neoclassical flavor was restricted to menswear. With the exception for some cadet uniforms, his proposals, and the similar suggestions of a number of other artists, were never instituted. Still, art historian and costume specialist Aileen Ribeiro has argued convincingly of the artist's influence on the fashions of his day, given his knowledge of antique costume, his documented interest in fashionable dress, and his artistic primacy at the time. In any case, the increasing informality of women's dress that was introduced by the politically fraught portrait of the French queen in the early 1780s was explicitly described in classical terms by the end of the eighteenth century. White, somewhat cylindrical gowns in lawn and mull were draped in styles *à la Diane*, *à la romaine*, *à la grec*, or more inclusively, *à l'antique*.

The painting of Mrs. John Birch by George Romney shown at left on page 13 also represents certain conventions of the classical style as a kind of fancy dress for portraiture. As in antiquity, the sitter wears a long dress over a sleeved underdress. But the artist's rendering of what would originally have been a woolen peplos is ambiguously attached at the shoulders without evidence of fibulae. There is no apoptygma, or overfold, although he has placed a deep crease above the sitter's knees at a position that approximates the tunic-length apoptygma seen in classical works. The underdress too, with its oddly draped sleeves, does not conform to the pinned or buttoned and split-seamed sleeves of a chiton. Instead, it is anchored with an armlet of pearls, half-hidden in a cuffed twist of fabric.

By the 1790s, fashionable women had put aside their *robes à la française*, *à la polonaise*, and *à l'anglais* for the neoclassical chemise. Although an explicit historicism was reflected in architecture and the decorative arts, classicizing elements in the attire of the Directoire and Empire periods

were coded. The chemise dress was related only through oblique references to any true classical model. In the painting titled *Portrait of a Young Woman in White*, illustrated at right on page 13, the sitter is dressed in high Empire-period style. Her hairstyle is *à l'antique*, and her plain mull shift has the raised waistline seam that has come to be identified with the period's classical silhouette. In this particular gown, narrow muslin bands of the underdress, which form the shoulder straps and bust support, are visible. The sheer mull, however, barely veils the subject's nipples. In a detail intended to suggest a chiton's buttoned shoulderline, her sleeve has been pinched up in a drape and anchored with a small button and two tassels. A fringed shawl resembling the ancient Greek himation wraps around her. The antique forms substantiated in Græco-Roman art, together with such reinvented styles of classical dress in the Directoire and Empire periods, have inspired the work of many designers of the twentieth century.

The twentieth century began with an S-curve silhouette, which showed the persistence of the emphatically corseted waistline that had characterized fashionable dress since the end of the Empire period. Although it had shifted in its placement, the modish waistline, from the 1820s onward, was predicated on a corset that pinched in the midriff to its smallest possible dimension.

Paul Poiret, French, 1880–1944. Photograph of Paul and Denise Poiret dressed for *Les Fêtes de Bacchus*, 1912. Cliché Bibliothèque Nationale de France, Paris

As such, the 1906 fashion for an uncorseted figure promoted by the French couturier Paul Poiret, seen in the photograph on page 14 with his wife Denise, was nothing short of revolutionary. The first gowns that he presented, unencumbered by corsets, were in a high-waisted, Directoire Revival silhouette. Although they supposedly referenced the neoclassical period, their acidic colors and exotic accessorization were as much about the voguish Orientalism and classical revivals seen in Sergei Diaghilev's Ballets Russe as they were about the earlier period of Greek revival in dress. Leon Bakst, Diaghilev's costume designer, arrayed the theater impresario's productions with fantastical exotic splendor, but in dances with classical themes, such as *Daphnis et Chloè*, *Narcisse*, or *L'Après midi d'un faune* shown below, his costumes appear to follow antique models more studiously, though with adumbrations of Empire style.

After decades of the structured figure, the presentation of a supple body was not seen to require decorative elaboration. Certainly, the performances of Isadora Duncan relied as much on the authenticity of her simple classical dress as it did on her avant-garde choreography to rationalize the exposure of her limbs. In the photograph of the dancer by Edward Steichen reproduced on page 16, Duncan is seen exultant and wearing a composite Græco-Roman ensemble. Her Greek

himation is draped over a wide-sleeved gown represented in Roman art, and of a style persistent in the Near and Middle East. This mixing of garment types and details is not uncommon and illustrates the merging of elements of classical attire over time with the dress of other cultures in which an economy of cut is the basis of garment construction.

The interest in styles of the East and of the antique was, therefore, not mutually exclusive in fashion. In fact, the end of the nineteenth century had paved the way for Poiret's radical innovation through styles intended for fashionable *déshabille*—teagowns, nightgowns, peignoirs, and other lingerie. Softly draped columnar silhouettes that were characterized as "exotic" had been introduced as appropriate for undress. With references to garment types from North Africa, the Near East, China, Japan, and sometimes to ancient Greece and Rome or medieval and early Renaissance models, the paradigm of the uncorseted body as a potentially fashionable ideal was represented in the wardrobe of the woman of style. However, until Poiret, it was limited to the intimate confines of her boudoir.

Like his contemporary Fortuny, Poiret explored both regional and antique dress types for an alternative approach to dressmaking. This strategy, a blending of the effects and structural approaches of Orientalist and Græco-Roman forms, contributed as significantly in its way to the history of modern dress as did his abandonment of the corset.

The costume of non-Western cultures is often based on the integrity of the textile. To avoid any waste that occurs through the cutting and shaping of garments with an anatomical fit, the textile is pinned, sewn, or tied into shape. As with the ancient Greeks, these traditions rely primarily on rectangles of cloth as the basic modules of their garments. Classical Hellenic dress was based on the manipulation of rectangles of cloth, the dimensions of which were determined by the proportions of the frame of the loom, shown on page 17 in the painting on a Greek vase. The loom, which could be of varying width and height, was strung with yarns weighted at the bottom. The weights were wrapped in the additional lengths of yarn and unwound as a portion of the panel was completed and rolled up on the bar at the top of the loom. Skill at the loom was one of the attributes of Athena, goddess of wisdom, and the importance of weaving in the life of a Greek woman was such that it appeared as the pivotal component in mythic narratives: Arachne, a skilled weaver undone by her hubris; Ariadne, the princess whose yarn led Theseus out of the Minotaur's labyrinth; and perhaps most culturally resonant, Penelope, the wife of Odysseus, who in the long absence of her husband undid her weaving each evening to fend off her suitors. The value and

significance of textiles to the ancient Greeks can be seen in descriptions by Herodotus, in which he invariably distinguishes the apparel of his subjects according to the inherent characteristics of the cloth—its color, fineness, and pattern.

This is not to suggest, however, that the many styles of Greek dress as three-dimensional forms were insignificant. In fact, the reverse is substantiated by the specificity of the nomenclature of garments in texts, and by the numerous variations seen in sculptures and in vase paintings. To the ancient Greeks, clothing as a bearer of identity—age, class, gender, profession, ethnicity—was especially explicit. It is only in the translations of ancient Greek texts that a simplification of the detailed designations of dress is generalized into chiton, chlamys, and himation, or even more simplistically, as robe, gown, and mantle. This descriptive reductivism is exacerbated further by the difficulty of associating literary texts with visual documents.

Attempts to understand historical Hellenic dress are confounded by the inability to link the vast amount of literary and visual evidence that survives. Fashion history sidesteps the problem entirely with its overly edited view of classical models. For twentieth-century designers, classical dress has been limited to a very few readily identifiable types. But long robes, short robes, open robes, closed robes, wide mantles, narrow mantles, tunics, trousers, fitted garments, ungirdled garments, and more occur in ancient Greek representations. They reveal the innumerable permutations of classical dress that have not been transmitted to fashion over time. Without debating the documentary validity of such representations, it is still evident that apparel in ancient Greece was subject to modifications and variations over centuries that affect even the most static and persistent traditions of dress. That contemporary designers appear to refer to less than a handful of these types suggests the abridged and selective nature of fashion history.

The clothes of the ancient Greeks were essentially whole pieces of cloth. As such, the most complex-seeming garment could be returned to its original form as a rectangle of fabric with the removal of a stitch or pin. Classical dress, therefore, could be submitted to the functionalist criteria of modernists: the attempt to pare all the expressive qualities of their work to the elements and processes of fabrication and signs of utility. Nowhere is the intersection of classical antiquity and modernist dress more apparent than in the relief made by Alix, later known as Madame Grès, for the 1939 World's Fair. Held in Flushing Meadows, New York, the international exposition focused on the optimistic possibilities of a future based on technological advance. Grès, who was among the

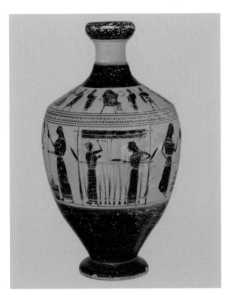

representatives of the haute couture, presented her gown in the trompe l'oeil classical relief seen at right on page 18. By presenting the gown in this state of partial completion (it can be seen in its completed state on page 41), Grès was able to convey the basis of her philosophy of dressmaking through the disclosure of her techniques and the process of her draping. The gown is seemingly composed of two parts, a bodice with peplum and a skirt, but it is actually draped of one continuous length of fabric. Like the apparel constructions of the ancient Greeks, Grès created the shaping of her gown through draping and cinching alone.

With similar affinities but a very different approach, Madeleine Vionnet worked with bias, the direction of the grain, or warp and weft of the fabric, aligning herself with both the ancient Greeks and the Italian Futurists. Vionnet worked on a half-sized mannequin set on a potter's wheel. For this reason, her designs can only be fully comprehended in the round. Like the conical construction of the peplos, her garments are fabrics wrapped around the body. Her dress pictured at right on page 18 is a simple bias tube, held together by a series of diamanté hooks like the pins on a chiton's sleeve. If the hooks were to be detached and the shoulders unstitched, the gown would dissolve into a flat piece of cloth. On the body, the gown's bias cut virtually precludes the wearing of undergarments, since it cleaves so closely to the female form. As the curator and costume historian Robert Riley noted, "In the 1920s, despite their bandeaus, the relief of a woman's nipples were often visible. But with the bias of the 1930s, it became possible to see the more shocking concavity of her navel."

Twentieth-century dress moved in a trajectory of increasing informality and, with the exception of the post-World-War-II period revival of waist cinching and hip padding, shifted toward a simplification in the shaping of pattern pieces that predicates the anatomical fit of clothes. In addition, a third, more erratically coursed trend was the growing expression of the natural body's form because of the advancing degree of socially permitted exposure. Although male nudity was an accepted part of Hellenic culture, dress for women was rather modest in its coverage, especially in public. Artistic depictions of women in light linen chitons, or even (although less plausibly) in woolen peploi convey the impression of an explicit disclosure of the body's contours that is inconsistent with other evidence of social convention. This and the representations of bared mortal and immortal female figures have contributed to the association of Greek dress with unselfconscious female nudity.

This celebration of the natural female form, together with the idea of apparel based on simple

geometries manipulated into diverse effects, made the dress of the ancient Greeks an apt paradigm for twentieth-century designers who were engaged by the strategies of modernism. That it also alluded to ancient myths and divinities allowed classicized dress to sustain, even expand, its influence on postmodernists, who could play with its compelling narratives. Of course, irony attaches to the phenomenon, since the system, driven by invention and an associated obsolescence, aspires to incorporate the imagery of a sustained and unchanging ideal. The strategy to submit ancient forms as modes of modernity and postmodernity, therefore, have not resulted in anything close to an archaeological or historical fidelity.

Classical allusions in fashionable dress have predated our contemporary expressions. If the evidence of art is to be relied on, components of classical attire have appeared throughout Western fashion's six-hundred-year history, although it is only from the 1790s to the 1810s that classicized forms have been embraced as a universal style. From then until the twentieth century, classical motives and references were essentially superficial. It was not until the movement to an uncorseted body was accomplished that classicism of the intensity of the Directoire and Empire periods could be recalled in fashion.

Above left: Madame Grès, French (1903–1993). Relief fragment created for the New York World's Fair, 1939. Photograph courtesy of Caroline Rennolds Milbank © Roger Viollet/Getty Images. Above right: Madeleine Vionnet, French (1876–1975). Evening gown, white satin and rhinestones, 1936. Photograph by George Hoyningen-Huene, Russian (1900–1968) courtesy of *Harper's Bazaar*

Even with the natural body's interregnum upon Christian Dior's reintroduction of the corset in 1947, couturiers continued to devise ways in which the softly draped aesthetic of classical dress could be introduced to their designs. It was not until the 1960s, however, with the move away from structured underpinnings, that fashions of a greater structural affinity to ancient precedents returned. In the 1967 photograph reproduced below, Mrs. Jacqueline Bouvier Kennedy on a visit to Cambodia wears a one-shouldered gown by Valentino derived from classical sources. In this context, Mrs. Kennedy looks like a Gandharan sculpture, in which Alexandrine Greek dress merges with Eastern iconography. Of seafoam green silk, it winds around her body like a Hellenic himation. Embroidered with a scalloped border of silver, pearls, and iridescent crystals, Valentino's creation recalls the fluted edges of a shell or the lapped rendering of waves in Botticelli's *Venus*. The classical allusion was not lost on the former First Lady, who as the wife of the President introduced symbolic connections between her dress and specific ceremonial functions. As Hamish Bowles observed in his catalogue for the Metropolitan Museum on her wardrobe from the Kennedy presidential years: "Mrs. Kennedy managed her public wardrobe as if she were a costume designer in theater or film; each outfit served to reinforce a point." Wrapped in silk like a wave, she alludes to

Aphrodite emerging from the foam of the sea, and to the classical affinities of the ancient dress forms of the region she was visiting.

The classical mode can be conveyed by a single detail or through an array of allusive effects. Most importantly, it is an alternative approach to the very creation of dress that frees the designer to transform the two-dimensional into the three-dimensional without resorting to the dressmaking conventions dependent on the shaped pattern piece. The costume of the ancient Greeks is a paradigm for the designer whose impulse is to make cloth into clothing with only the most minimal of interventions. In the end, with its aura of mythic beauty sustained over time, the classical mode is nothing less than the desire to transfigure women into goddesses.

Valentino Garavani, Italian (born 1932). Evening gown, green silk with pearl and crystal beads, 1967. Photograph of Jacqueline Onassis on official business in Cambodia by Larry Burrows, courtesy of Archivio Valentino

PANDORA'S BOX: THE CHITON, PEPLOS, AND HIMATION

In the absence of any surviving clothing, art and literature provide the only evidence of classical dress, opening a Pandora's Box of confusion and contradiction. The apparel of ancient Greece was, even in its own day, subject to numerous modifications and transformations. In the huge variety of costumes delineated in artworks and categorized by scholars, exceptions are rife and consistency is elusive. Because specialists of the high classical period of ancient Greece have developed terminology based on a variety of methodologies—art historical, archaeological, and literary—certain discrepancies are perhaps inevitable. However, in every instance, the glossaries are also a simplified system, identifying numerous and specific forms of dress under quite general labels. In this book, the nomenclature is simplified even further, originating from the structure of the garment rather than from any other criteria.

The diversity of women's apparel in ancient Greece can be reduced to three general garment types: the chiton, the peplos, and the himation—which are discussed and illustrated in the glossary at the back of this volume.

Structurally, the most elemental dress type is the chiton, which is constructed in several ways. The most commonly represented is accomplished by stitching two rectangular pieces of fabric together along either sideseam, from top to bottom, forming a cylinder with its top edge and hem unstitched. The top edges are then sewn, pinned, or buttoned together at two or more points to form shoulder seams, with reserve openings for the head and arms.

The peplos is perhaps a more distinctively Greek garment than the chiton, insofar as the chiton's reductive construction has similarities to apparel types in a number of other cultures and times. However, the peplos has several characteristics that distinguish it from other clothing traditions. Made of one large rectangular piece of cloth, it was formed into a cylinder and then folded along the topline into a deep cuff, creating an apoptygma, or capelet-like overfold. Although there are exceptional instances of chitons represented with overfolds, a garment is not a peplos unless it has been draped with an apoptygma. The neckline and armholes of the peplos were formed by fibulae, brooch-like pins that attached the back to the front of the garment at either shoulder. Of any of the identifying characteristics of a peplos, the fastening of its shoulders with fibulae is its single defining detail.

While there are a number of scarf, veil, shawl, and mantle forms, all with distinct nomenclature, it is the himation, with its range of draping and wrapping possibilities, that has been the most evident source of later evocations of Hellenic dress. The himation was a large cloak, always orthogonal, unlike the Roman toga, which had some shaping. Like the toga, however, it appears to have had a variety of cultural meanings, depending on its proportion and how it was worn. Generally, when worn by women, it was a garment of decorous modesty, but it has been shown on hetærae as a device for provocation.

The diminishing number of paradigmatic Grecian dress types belies the artistic and literary evidence. But it may be that in the narrowing of types, their potency as carriers of ideals of the antique became even more concentrated over time. It is in the variation and manipulation of a reduced number of basic iconic styles that later artists and contemporary designers have been able to expand on their increasingly inventive interpretations of Grecian dress.

The most typical forms of classical dress are represented in a scene of Persephone's return to her mother, the goddess Demeter. Persephone has been led out of Hades by Hermes and Hekate, and is seen emerging out of the earth wearing a himation over her pleated linen chiton. Hermes wears the abbreviated chlamys and short chiton characteristic of male attire. Hekate, carrying two torches, is dressed in an open-sided peplos. The scene is surveyed by Demeter who, like Persephone, wears a himation over her chiton. In ancient Greece, the three basic elements of female dress—the chiton, peplos, and himation—could be worn in various configurations through different methods of draping. Belting and harnessing were the mechanisms for transforming the essentially static construction and configuration of the chiton and peplos. Many of the variations accomplished through these methods became codified, and persisted as preferred styles for centuries. The Greek historian Herodotus referred to dress as an expression of Greek identity that served as a signifier of Hellenic cultural authority in the ancient world. That it continues to do so in the collections of contemporary fashion designers suggests the potency of this apparently delimited range of garment types as a carrier of identity and ideology.

Greek (Attic), attributed to the Persephone Painter. *The Return of Persephone*, terracotta bell-krater, ca. 440 B.C. The Metropolitan Museum of Art, Fletcher Fund, 1928 (28.57.23)

Milanese designer Romeo Gigli is known for combining supple and sensuous draping with strictly controlled tailoring. Gigli's interest in the juxtaposition of ease and constraint is seen here in his updated version of a linen chiton. While conforming in most regards to its antique precedent, with its shift-like cut and simple blouson waist, the dress differs subtly in Gigli's introduction of slight shaping at the armhole. At the same time, Gigli severely narrows the hemline of the chiton of antiquity, a garment that allowed for considerable freedom of movement. Generally, a chiton of shorter length, a chitoniskos, is characteristic of the style worn by men in ancient Greece and, when associated with the female sex, by the Greek goddess Artemis or the Amazons, the mythic foreign tribe of warrior women.

Isadora Duncan, the pioneer of American modern dance, rejected the constraints of traditional ballet technique and costuming. She devised her own free style based on natural movement, and performed in modern versions of classical dress. Duncan danced barefoot without the benefit of flesh-toned tights, scandalizing and titillating the public with her artistic, classically rationalized semi-nudity. Her costumes were often scraps of silk, attached by knotting or safety pins and tied with cords or later, elastic bands. As the sketch on the left shows, Duncan infused her dance with the wild delirium of the maenads, the women in Greek mythology who were votaries of Dionysos, the god of wine. Captured mid-leap, Duncan transformed herself into a modern maenad by donning a revealing version of a chiton. Her ecstatic choreography is alluded to in Lamsweerde and Matadin's photograph of contemporary designer Hussein Chalayan's white shift, shown on the following two pages. Unlike Duncan's interpretation of the classical chiton, with its high Empire waistline, Chalayan's design controls the fullness at the lower hip. Still, Chalayan has achieved an effect similar to that of the dancer's more historical rendering by inserting tabs at the side seams that pull in and cradle the bust, with an effect like the one achieved by the muslin supports in the chemises of early-nineteenth-century Empire-period fashions.

In this Roman copy of a Greek original, Eirene, one of the three Horai or Seasons, wears a peplos. The defining structural elements of a peplos are its point of attachment at the shoulder with a fibula, and its apoptygma which partially, and sometimes fully, covered the torso. A peplos of great fullness and length such as this one was appropriate for a deity, as an explicit expression of abundance, dignity, and prestige. Here, the gown is hitched up with a single girdle at the waist, creating a deep kolpos that peeks out from under the apoptygma. The peplos was formed by folding a large rectangle in half, with the fold at the left side. The edges of the cloth at the right side were either sewn together to form a sideseam or left open to fall in a fluted drape. Eirene is depicted with a peplos in the fashion of the former construction, with the right side stitched closed.

As exemplified by the illustration on the following two pages, the late-nineteenth-century history painter Sir Lawrence Alma-Tadema specialized in depicting scenes of everyday life in ancient Greece and Rome. Alma-Tadema's successful evocation of classical antiquity relied greatly on the scholarship of his time. Like many artists working in a tradition of historical subjects, the authority of his paintings was judged in part by the sense of scholarship and verisimilitude conveyed by elements of architecture, decoration, and costume. For instance, the painting shown here describes a symposium, or gathering for entertainment. The maiden plays a diaulos, or double flute, and like Eirene, she wears a peplos, although unlike the goddess's, hers is open-sided. In a small deviation from ancient Greek practice, the artist reversed the lapping of the peplos' shoulder. His fibula pins the front shoulder piece over the back rather than the back over front, as seen in historical representations.

Left: *Eirene, Daughter of Zeus and Themis*, marble, Roman copy of a Greek original of the 4th century B.C. The Metropolitan Museum of Art, Rogers Fund, 1906 (06.311). Overleaf: Sir Lawrence Alma-Tadema (1863–1912). *The Siesta* (detail), oil on canvas, 1868. © Museo Nacional del Prado, Madrid

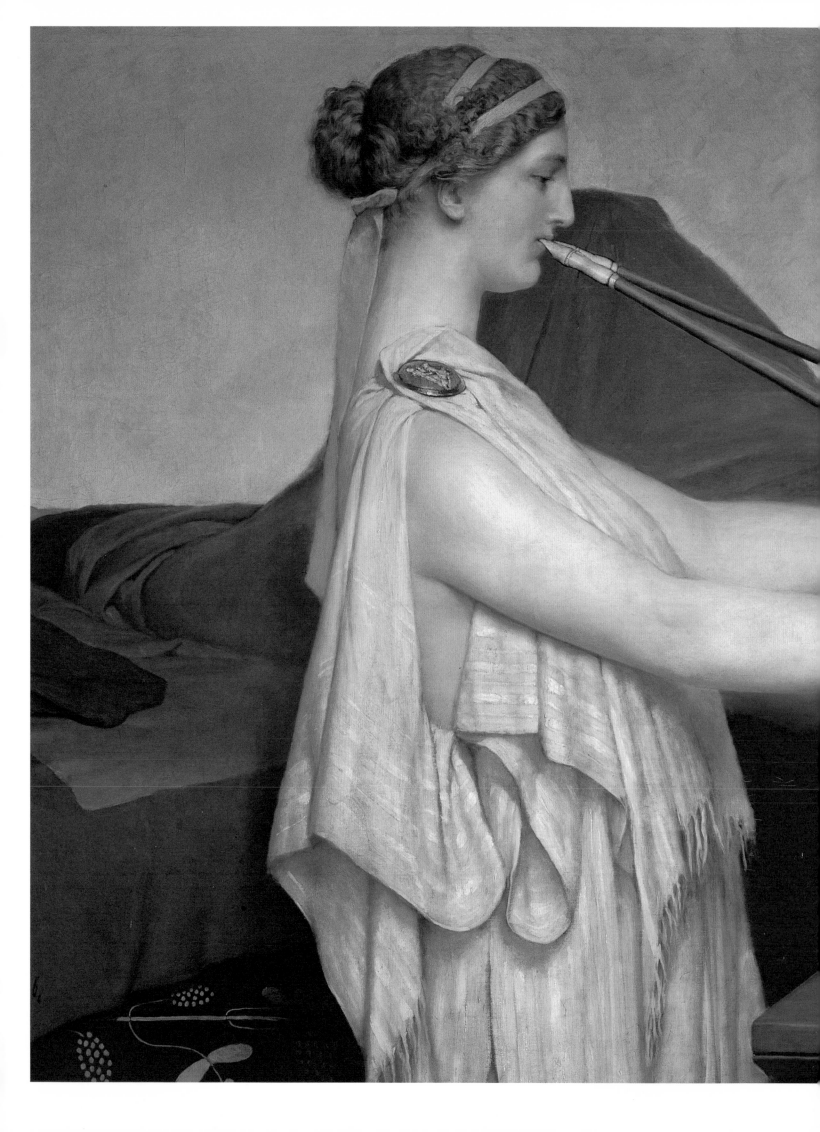

During the first decade of the twentieth century, Paul Poiret initiated a fashion sea-change when he declared the wasp-waisted silhouette outmoded, and the columnar form of high-waisted Directoire-Revival gowns the vogue. This jettisoning of the corset alone established Poiret as among the most important and influential designers to this day. In this two-piece dinner gown, Poiret's interest in the "liberating" style and cut of non-Western regional dress results in a peplos-like ensemble. Two separate but identical squares of cloth, one worn like a short poncho and the other wrapped into a cylindrical skirt, create a peplos effect with its apoptygma-style top. Although the ensemble is not constructed like any classical Greek precedent, the use of cloth, completely orthogonal as if off the loom, suggests an affinity to the simply configured garments of the ancient world, which were also formed out of rectilinear pieces of cloth scaled to their intended use directly on the loom. This interest in the non-tailored traditions of much regional dress was not restricted to Poiret, nor was his conflation of classical styles with ethnographic forms. Madame Grès is perhaps the best example of the phenomenon, but Cristobal Balenciaga, Valentino, Issey Miyake, and Romeo Gigli, among others, have all made Græco-Roman allusions through minimalist constructions based on clothing traditions outside the Western fashion system.

Paul Poiret, French (1880–1944). Dinner dress, navy-blue and red silk faille, and gold metallic bullion buttons, 1922–1923. The Metropolitan Museum of Art, The Costume Institute, Gift of Mrs. Muriel Draper, 1943 (CI 43.85.2a, b)

In this fashion plate from 1920, the illustrator André Marty transposed a form of Grecian dress to a Moroccan seraglio. Except for its length, the garment is rendered with all the attributes of an ancient peplos. In the popular imagination, vestiges of classical and biblical dress were thought to persist in the styles of North Africa and the Middle East, since vernacular dress from those regions shared the loosely draped and untailored construction of antique styles. This fanciful depiction of a fatma, in this context a Muslim woman, shows her preparing to girdle her waist, as was the practice with the Grecian peplos. In the instance of the ancient style, the girdling served to raise the hem of the skirt, which on a fully cut gown would otherwise have dragged on the ground. Here, it is unclear whether the fatma in her "improvisation" is intending to cinch in the waist of her dress over or under her apoptygma-like overfold. In classical Greece, the general practice was to girdle the waist under the overfold, although there are many examples in which the cinching occurs over the apoptygma.

André Marty, French. "Les Beaux Jours de Fez ou La Fatma Improvisée," illustrated in *Gazette du Bon Ton*, April 1920, plate 16. The Metropolitan Museum of Art, The Irene Lewisohn Costume Reference Library, Woodman-Thompson Collection

LES BEAUX JOURS DE FEZ
ou
LA FATMA IMPROVISÉE

The Greek goddess Nike, the mythological personification of victory in sport and war, was called Victoria by the Romans. In his figure *Victory*, the American sculptor Augustus Saint-Gaudens girdled her peplos over her apoptygma to create a "peplum." This short skirt-like hem of the cinched apoptygma could vary in length, depending on the dimension of the peplos itself. If the peplos was very long, a wider apoptygma could be formed, and consequently a deeper peplum. In classical depictions, whenever belted in this fashion, the apoptygma is generally shown ending at the hipline, although there are many instances where the peplum extends down to mid-thigh. Sometimes the cinched apoptygma conveys the impression that the peplos is composed of a separate belted tunic and underdress or skirt.

Augustus Saint-Gaudens, American (1848–1907). *Victory*, gilt bronze, 1912–1916, reduction of figure from The Sherman Monument, Grand Army Plaza, New York City, 1903. The Metropolitan Museum of Art, Purchase: Rogers Fund, 1917 (17.90.1)

This photograph by George Platt Lynes features a dress by Madame Grès, who was known earlier as Alix. The model raises a chiffon stole in a pose like that of a maenad, a votary of Dionysos. The classical converges with the surreal in the setting, a Yves Tanguy-like landscape with an attenuated and faintly distorted figure. The dramatic highlighting and moody silhouette give the dress the look of a sculptural relief. Like many of the draped silk-jersey gowns with which Grès is identified, this evening gown substantiates the designer's classicizing intentions and antique sources. Like the overgirdled apoptygma on Augustus Saint-Gaudens's *Victory*, her creation has a small peplum. In addition, she introduced pleating to the center-front of the gown. For Grès, pleating was a means of fitting a garment without pattern-shaping and seaming. Like the ancient Greeks, she preferred an economy of line. And when she could, she avoided the cutting of fabric, relying instead on the bias and pleating to establish the shaping of her garments.

Dress: Madame Grès, French (1903–1993). Evening gown with peplum, silk jersey, 1940. Photograph: George Platt Lynes, American (1907–1955), gelatin silver print, 1940. The Metropolitan Museum of Art, Purchase: David Hunter McAlpin Fund, 1941 (41.65.2). Permission courtesy of George P. Lynes, II, Executor, Estate of George Platt Lynes

The two girls depicted in this funerary monument suggest the problematic nature of contemporary identifications of classical dress. The young woman on the right wears a peplos over a chiton. Additionally, she has pinned to her shoulders a short mantle that falls down her back. In ancient Greek times, fabric for any article of clothing was woven only to the dimensions required to avoid cutting or waste. An excess of fabric in the chiton of an adult woman, which would have to be hitched up in a kolpos, signified wealth and prestige. However, because the young woman has not made a kolpos, her apoptygma is particularly long. When seen in marble, the overfold, whether on a peplos or more rarely on a chiton, is easily interpreted as a separate garment. The young girl on the left wears a similar garment. However, it appears to be structured like a chiton with sewn shoulder seams, and an apoptygma characteristic of a peplos. While examples of this type appear on adult women, its construction is especially appropriate to a child. Unstitched, the chiton's atypical overfold could accommodate a child's growth. It is possible that the belief that tunic dresses were a popular classical style was inspired by a misreading of sculptural representations, together with the existence of depictions of tunic ensembles in artworks, often as attire for special occasions or the dress of non-Greeks.

Greek (Attic). Statue of a young woman from marble grave monument, ca. 320 B.C. The Metropolitan Museum of Art, Rogers Fund, 1944 (44.11.2, 3)

Although depictions of figures wearing tunics over their chitons are not unknown in ancient art, they are the exception rather than the rule. Examples sometimes appear in representations of Athena, in which she is shown dressed in an astrochiton, a short sleeveless overtunic patterned with stars. Based on the evidence of ancient artworks, it was common practice to don a peplos over a chiton, but the pairing of an overtunic with a coordinated underdress did not appear with any comparable frequency. Joseph-Marie Vien, a French neoclassical painter, is best remembered as the teacher of Jacques-Louis David. In his painting of a pious Athenian shown on the right, she is dressed in a long tunic over a chiton that is split at either side, exposing her legs to mid-thigh. This glimpse of the bare leg suggests the eighteenth-century use of classical themes to rationalize an erotic allure, an opportunity for legitimized exposure of the body. In numerous other examples, Vien dressed his figures similarly in costumes of his own invention. The single button fastening at either shoulder suggests the use of fibulae on a peplos rather than the stitched or multiple button and pin fastenings of the chiton. This small detail and the larger reformulations of classical dress that appear in his work are representative of the way antique models have been subjected to fantastical permutations by later artists.

Joseph-Marie Vien, French (1716–1809). *The Virtuous Athenian*, oil on canvas, 18th century. Musée des Beaux Arts de Strasbourg. Photograph: A. Plisson

(16.)

Diadême de Roses. Tunique de Bal.

Neubauer sculp: à Francfort s/m

What painters, sculptors, and designers of fancy dress in the eighteenth century and earlier fabricated as the dress of the antique became the prevailing fashion in the era of neoclassical revivalism. This evening toilette from 1802 documents the shift from the artistic imagination of the eighteenth century to the fashion of the salon and the street of the early nineteenth century. In this ballgown *à la grec*, the tunic falls asymmetrically off the left shoulder, alluding to the undone chitons of ancient art that bared the breasts of Amazons and goddesses. The draping of the sleeve and the hem of the skirt are caught up by roses—not an original attribute of Aphrodite, the goddess of love, but one that became identified with her. The deep asymmetrical folds that result allude to the draped swags associated with antique statuary.

Raymond Duncan, the brother of Isadora, was always a fervent advocate of classical dress. So fanatical was his belief in the healthfulness of Grecian styles that Duncan had his son walk through Central Park in mid-winter clad only in a short chiton, chlamys, and sandals—an incident for which he was charged with the endangerment of a child. In ancient Greece, women were more substantially covered than men. A sleeveless woolen peplos or, as in the dress shown here, a tunic could be donned over a sleeved or sleeveless linen chiton. For this ensemble designed for his wife, Duncan hand-painted the overtunic. In place of a chiton, he substituted a similarly constructed but wider chiffon underdress. The pairing of an opaque tussah silk and a sheer chiffon is more evocative of nineteenth-century artistic conceits than it is of any antique Hellenic evidence. In addition, the pattern of the tunic is more closely aligned with the taste of the early-twentieth-century Aesthetic Movement than it is with the patterns from classical Greece. The apples, grapes, and leaves, with their faint evocation of Dionysian pastoralism, are rendered in the Arts and Crafts style.

Raymond Duncan, American (1874–1966). Ensemble, tussah silk with polychrome hand-painted vegetal motif and wood beads, navy-blue silk chiffon, 1920s.

The Metropolitan Museum of Art, The Costume Institute, Purchase: Isabel Shults Fund, 1990 (1990.152)

In the sculpture on the facing page, Artemis—the Greek name for Diana, goddess of the hunt—is depicted fastening a himation over her double-girdled chiton. The himation has been doubled over to form an abbreviated cloak, more in the proportion of the Greek man's chlamys than with the fuller blanket-like scale of a woman's wrap. Additionally, the goddess has transformed her own feminine garment into the proportions of the shorter male chiton. The cinching of her chiton signifies the goddess's requirement for freedom of movement in the hunt. The deep kolpos indicates that her chiton has been hitched up at least a foot. Undone, it would almost reach her ankles.

The Isadora Duncan-style dancers shown on the following two pages have adopted the shorter chiton style of the Artemis statue. But they conform to ancient Greek convention in their use of more capacious and consequently more modest himations. In both the classical artwork and the modernist dance, dress is an opportunity for the exposure of the female form. In the antique depiction, the virgin goddess, never seen by mortals with impunity, is caught unaware, her chiton slipping off her shoulders, and her legs bared. The healthful exposure of the early-twentieth-century "Isadorables" is rationalized through such ancient precedent.

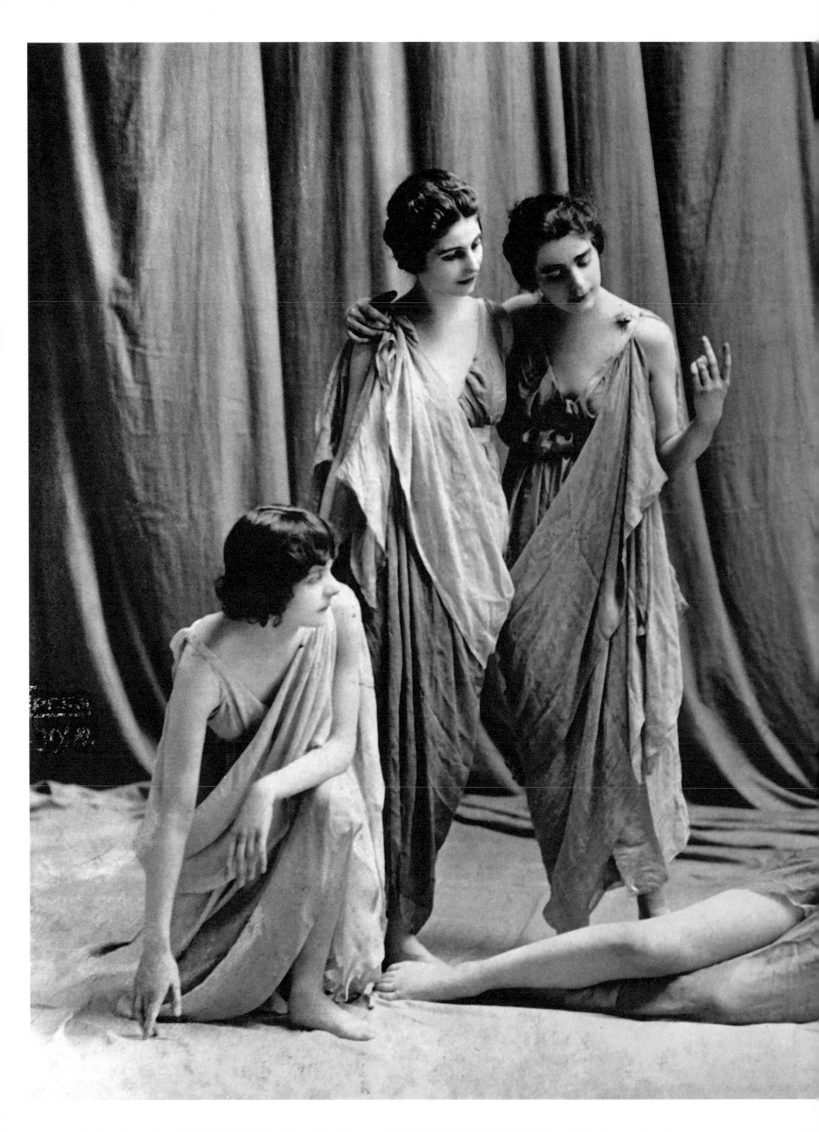

A number of fashion designers have referenced the reduced scale of Artemis's himation, which was folded over into the style of a man's chlamys. As shown on the facing page, Mariano Fortuny printed a velvet rectangle intended to be worn as a mantle, and fastened the shoulder with a Venetian glass bead. Similarly, Madame Grès took a square of velvet to knot at the shoulder, but also to wrap around the waist as a sarong. Both Fortuny and Grès kept to the notion of the short chlamys-like himation as a separate element of dress. More recent designers have taken the effect of the overmantle and incorporated it into the construction of the gown itself. In her minidress seen on the left on the following page, Jean Muir, known for her supple drapes and minimal cuts in silk and wool jersey, evoked the silhouette of an ancient Greek man dressed in chlamys and short chiton rather than the modestly covered form that would characterize any Greek woman. As shown in her designs at right on the next page, Donna Karan alluded to philosophical and spiritual themes in recent collections. Her ivory palette of luxurious silks and experimental gauzes underscores the vestal-like ethereality of her subtly draped dresses with chlamys- and himation-scaled volume.

Left: Mariano Fortuny, Italian (born Spain 1871–1949). Chlamys, brown and gray silk velvet printed with metallic silver; Dress: rust pleated silk, early 20th century. Chlamys: Courtesy Mark Walsh, Yonkers, New York; Dress: The Metropolitan Museum of Art, The Costume Institute, Gift of Clare Fahnestock Moorehead, 2001 (2001.702a). Right: Madame Grès, French (1903–1993). Evening gown, green silk jersey and green silk velvet, 1978. The Metropolitan Museum of Art, The Costume Institute, Gift of Chessy Rayner, 1997 (1997.116.1a, b). Overleaf left: Jean Muir, British (1928–1995). Dress, red silk jersey, ca. 1980. Courtesy of Sandy Schreier. Overleaf center: Donna Karan, American (born 1948). Evening dress, white synthetic "techno gauze," spring–summer 2002. Overleaf right: Donna Karan. Evening gown, white silk satin, spring–summer 2002. Courtesy of Donna Karan New York

This alluring little Greek bronze from the Hellenistic period portrays an entertainer—part mime, part dancer—swathed in a voluminous himation. So light is her mantle that the folds and drape of her peplos appear from below in relief. While the shawl-like himation was considered obligatory for the public appearance of any respectable Greek matron, its enhancement of the voluptuous movements of the dancer suggests its ability to convey meanings beyond a dignified propriety and modesty. The scale of the himation and the quality of its weight and weave communicated wealth, prestige, and luxury. Its function as a status symbol was directly related to its quality and amplitude. In the evening ensemble by Halston illustrated on the following two pages, a double-tiered cape functions in the same way as the classical himation. The cape is composed of several layers and many yards of silk chiffon. With its allusion to the regular folds of antique dress, the pleating consumes an especially large amount of fabric. The simply constructed cape could be worn in a variety of ways, but it always provides decorous coverage for the bare gown beneath. Also pleated, the travertine-colored halter gown with a plunging neckline and completely bared back is essentially a fluted Greek column.

Right: Greek. *Veiled and Masked Dancer*, bronze, ca. 250–220 B.C. The Metropolitan Museum of Art, Bequest of Walter C. Baker, 1971 (1972.118.95).

Overleaf: Halston (Roy Halston Frowick), American (1932–1990). Evening gown and wrap (two views), pleated ivory and beige silk chiffon, 1974.

The Metropolitan Museum of Art, The Costume Institute, Gift of Hillie (Mrs. David) Mahoney, 1996 (1996.498.2a, b)

In this Roman copy after an ancient Greek original, the chiton and himation of Artemis are modified to accommodate the freedom of movement required for the rigors of the hunt. Her ankle-length chiton is hitched above her waist into a full kolpos. The copyist has deflated the blouson, perhaps misreading it as the hem of a short tunic. The goddess is depicted in mid-chase with her himation twisted into a long sash draped diagonally across her shoulder and around her waist. The himation is rarely seen this way, as a narrowed coil of fabric. Its expanse is generally regarded as a virtue, and it is most commonly shown in its unfurled state, billowing in the wind or cocooning the head and body in a shroud-like wrap. Worn across the torso in this fashion rather than in the more popular mode as a wide mantle, the manipulated himation inspires for designers a series of variations on what is ultimately a simple rectangle of cloth straight from the loom.

Pierre Cardin's short cocktail dress was described in *Vogue* as a "little Greek one-shoulder dress in white crepe with folds of bias drapery thrown across the top." The dress is unlike any antique garment, though its combination of one-shoulder neckline, white color, and drapery evokes a classical style. The 1960s are remembered primarily for the crisp architectonic cuts of Cardin and Emanuel Ungaro that had a space-age modernity. But the decade also saw a proliferation of minimally constructed shifts that referred not to the promise of a high-tech future but to the utopian arcadia of the classical past. The impulse to classicism, with its reliance on elastic materials and draping rather than complicated cuts, was popularly adopted in lingerie and ready-to-wear. In its manifestations in the couture, however, the most basic effects were often the consequence of sophisticated constructions. Here, the apparently simple adumbration of Artemis's rolled himation is a deep bias cuff that is cut as part of the fitted bodice pieces. The one-shouldered drape that appears to be a separate applied element is instead a continuous cowl.

Pierre Cardin, French (born 1922). Evening dress, white crepe with black patent-leather belt, spring–summer 1969. Photograph by Bert Stern courtesy of *Vogue*

The collections of Madame Grès were prized for the pleated silk jersey gowns that ended each of her shows. With their himation-like draped swags, these designs are a relaxed version of the fine dense pleating that generally covers her fitted highly structured bodices. In both examples shown here, as in all her signature work, the technical virtuosity incorporated in the draping is revealed only on close study. The swags are both continuous and unbroken panels of fabric that incorporate the right fronts and backs of the gowns. In her neoclassicism, Grès conformed to the antique notion of uninterrupted lengths of cloth, stitched but not cut into shape. From her earliest work, Grès introduced windows onto the body with cutouts that bared the back and midriff. For the gown on the left of the facing page, she created a fissured shoulder, consistent with her own practice and resonant of the split shoulderlines of antique chitons. The dense draping of the handkerchief-weight jersey in the gown to the right provides carefully positioned coverage. At either side of the hips and legs, however, only a taut layer of fabric is provided for a sensuous disclosure of the body's contours.

Isadora Duncan is shown to the right wearing a long-sleeved underdress, a t-shaped form of the chiton not unknown to the Greeks but commonly associated with the Romans, for whom it persisted as a basic clothing type for centuries. More idiosyncratic is the legendary dancer's method of draping her himation. For her dance *Aulis*, Duncan concocted a novel method of wrapping the long garment. She threw one end of the rectangular mantle over her right shoulder, then draped it diagonally across her front and around her back, and finally anchored the other end with a fibula-like button on her left shoulder. Interesting interpretations in the draping of the himation abound, but the crisscrossing of the mantle over the body had particular resonance for the late 1920s and the 1930s, when the use of fabric on the bias prevailed. By positioning the fabric diagonally, the warp and weft of the cloth is turned into true bias, an angle of increased elasticity. The bias allows unstitched cloth to fall in supple folds, and when incorporated into a pattern-piece, it creates a body-cleaving tautness. On the overleaf are a photograph and its reverse by the surrealist artist Man Ray, showing a dress by Madame Grès. She exploited the natural elasticity of silk jersey, a knit, and she also disposed her panels in the fashion of Duncan, thus introducing additional contouring to her fluid design. Known for her interest in the classical past, Grès evoked ancient Greek precedent in the continuous unbroken wrap of her pattern-pieces. It is as if she melded the diagonal of a himation into the body of a chiton, without color or pattern as in the scoured marbles of antiquity.

As exemplified to the right, classical references have recurred in Alexander McQueen's eponymous collections, as they have in his work for Givenchy Haute Couture. McQueen's women are often heroic, but with vestiges of some prior violence they have endured and overcome. His juxtaposition of vulnerability and strength, victimization and transcendence, is reflected in the materials as much as in the components of his designs. In this example, fragile chiffon scarves are overlayed across a short dress in the "X" of Isadora Duncan's himation, shown on page 69. With fabric stitched like wet drapery onto a protective breastplate-like corset, the wearer becomes a contemporary Nike. And with the shredded ends of her chiton and himation, she alludes to a victorious emergence from a battle at sea. The narrow lengths of cloth that come to represent the more expansive himation are perhaps a misreading of the edges of the billowing sail-like himation of a maenad, a follower of Dionysos. In the marble relief depicting three maidens on overleaf one, the edges of their wind-blown mantles appear to be almost scarf-like forms. By the eighteenth century, the himation not only narrowed and attenuated, it also took on a gossamer insubstantiality. Elihu Vedder's painting of the Pleiades shown on overleaf two and George Hoyningen-Huene's photograph of evening pajamas by Madeleine Vionnet shown on overleaf three both include long shawls and bias sashes that established a classicizing intention and allusion.

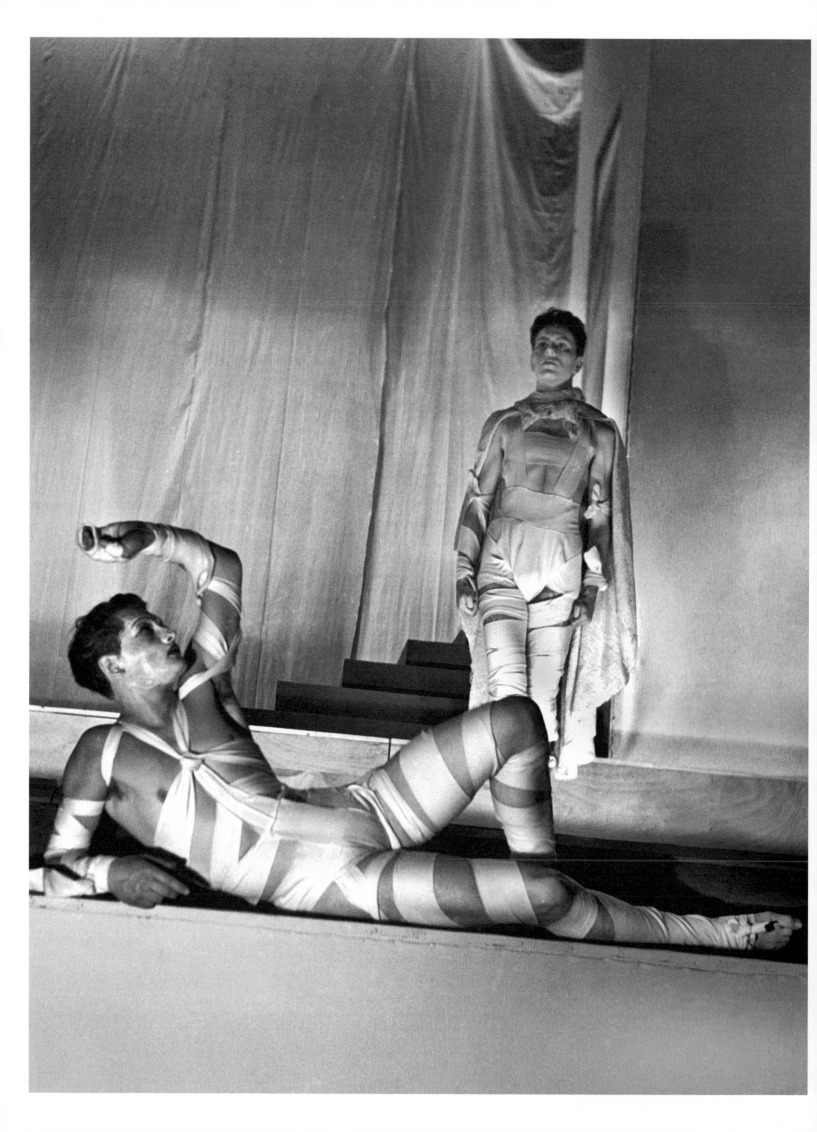

In addition to her famed work in high fashion, Gabrielle "Coco" Chanel also designed stage costumes for such plays as Jean Cocteau's *Antigone* (1923) based on the ancient tragedy by Sophocles. Chanel confounded and scandalized the audience of Cocteau's *Oedipus Rex* (1937), with her bandage-like costumes for the male roles. Her association of classicism with the criss-cross harnessing of Greek dress and with the lacing of classical footwear established a new model for the antique. In this photograph, showing the famed actor Jean Marais as Oedipus, the costuming recalls what one writer has described as Cocteau's "skeletal version of Sophocles' original." Chanel herself flirted with the most reductive elements of dress—mundane cloths and the most basic cuts—in some of her iconic designs. With a modernist's strategy, she extrapolated one element of classical dress—the ancient practice of wrapping rather than tailoring cloth to fit the body—and expanded it into a semaphore.

Gabrielle Chanel, French (1883–1971). Costumes for *Oedipus Rex*, libretto and direction by Jean Cocteau (1889–1963), 1937. Photograph of actor Jean Marais by Lipnitzki © Roger Viollet/Getty Images

Halston called these dresses his "Goddess" gowns. His goddesses, however, were the stars of Hollywood, Broadway, and American high society. In creating dresses for his celebrity clients, Halston balanced his impulse to minimalism with an ingenious ability to infuse his work with glamour. Styles that recalled the antique through the filter of 1930s silver-screen sirens appeared with regularity in his collections. Halston was a master of simple constructions with maximum effects. His Goddess gowns typify his best work, alluding both to the scarf ties of Vionnet and the bandage wrapping of Chanel. Comprised of two long sash-like bands attached at the waist to a floor-length skirt, they could not be more basic in form. However, as in the variety available to the ancient Greeks, the gowns can be worn in a number of ways—as a halter, or with the bands criss-crossing at the back and across the midriff. Made of pliable silk jersey, the bands mold to the torso, while the skirt falls into undulating folds. Although far removed from any Greek precedent, the bands are an evolved and morphed form that conflates a misreading of the classical himation with the harnesses used to control the fullness of the chiton.

Halston (Roy Halston Frowick), American (1932–1990). Two "Goddess" gowns, ca. 1972. Left: blue silk jersey; right: brown silk jersey. Lent by The Museum at The Fashion Institute of Technology, New York, Gift of Lauren Bacall (76.69.17; 76.118.3)

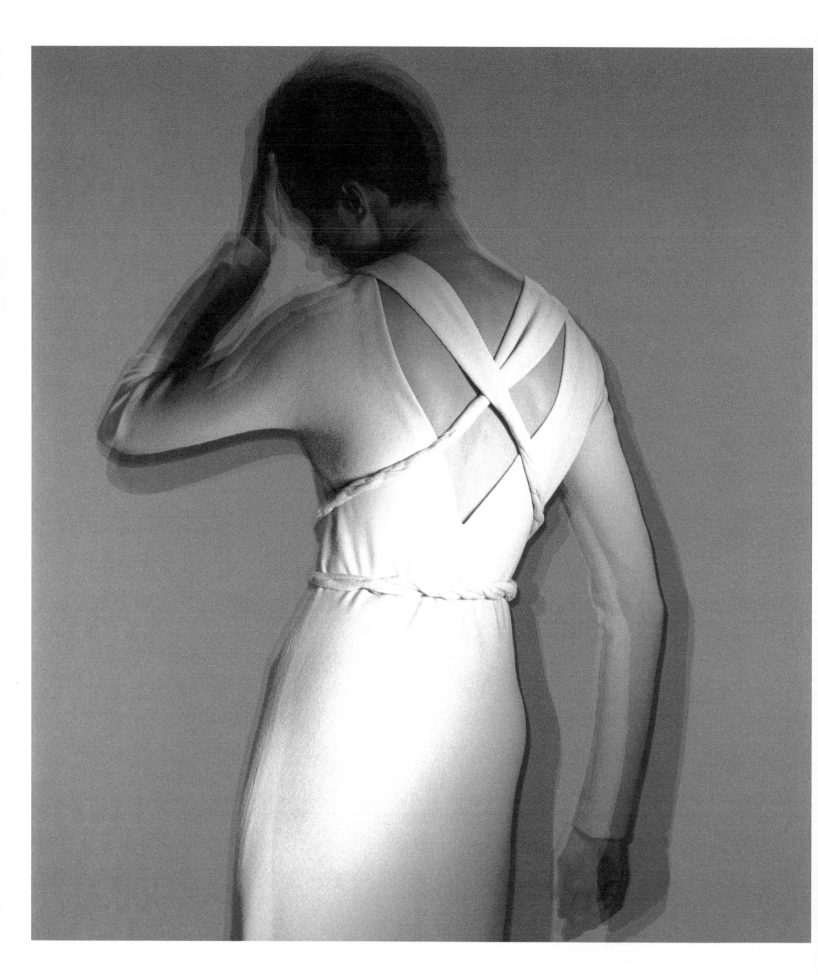

In ancient Greece, the amplitude of garments was controlled by girdles and harnesses. The latter Hellenic practice of harnessing the chiton is best seen on the sculpture *Charioteer of Delphi*, shown on page 12. He wears a figure-eight shoulder harness which pulls in the fullness of his sleeves in a raglan line at front and in a criss-cross at back. Geoffrey Beene's design gives the classical harness a literal modernist twist. The harness becomes an integral part of the garment it controls. And, as in much of his work, the revealed structure functions as a decorative flourish. Beene's economy of cut belies the sophistication of his technique and the complexity of his thought. Although he has omnivorous cultural interests, Beene rarely cites other cultures or the past in ways that are easily recognizable. Where such references occur, they appear so consonant with his own aesthetic leitmotifs that it is difficult to determine their source or the designer's narrative intention. The harness is such a motif. It recurs in different forms throughout his work, sometimes resembling the shoulderstrap of a holster, sometimes a surgical sling, and sometimes, as here, the corded bindings of ancient dress.

Geoffrey Beene, American (born 1927). Dress, cream wool jersey, spring–summer 1995. Photograph: Hiro Studio

Tom Ford's recent designs suggest an atavistic Hellenism that resembles the costumes by Dionyssis Fotopoulos for the Michael Cacoyannis film *Iphigenia*. The gown shown here is seemingly shredded and pulled asunder, like the rent vestige of a garment. That Ford treated silk chiffon with such atypical roughness introduces a further sense of physical excess, even violence, to his design. Well-versed in contemporary art and architecture, he applied the deconstructivist strategy of exposing points of structural destabilization in this gown for Yves Saint Laurent Rive Gauche. By doing so, he revealed the intrinsic components of the gown's making: narrow cords like Grecian harnesses and bands of fabric draped rather than shaped by cutting to fit the contours of the body. Pictured on the cover of *Time* as the "Dress of the Year," Ford's gown, reduced to narrow raw-edged bands of chiffon, established a new paradigm for the venerable House of Saint Laurent. Fashion's classicism was shifted into a more elemental and primitivistic phase.

Yves Saint Laurent Rive Gauche, French (founded 1966), by Tom Ford, American (born 1961). Evening gown, brown silk chiffon, spring–summer 2002.

Courtesy of Yves Saint Laurent Rive Gauche

THE METAMORPHOSES: CLASSICAL TRANSFORMATIONS
AND CONTEMPORARY PERMUTATIONS

The richness and variety of the costumes represented in ancient Greek art are often the result of simple manipulations of the three basic garment types: the chiton, the peplos, and the himation. Positioning a waist cinch or a shoulder harness and removing a fibula introduced to the ancient wardrobe the possibility of innumerable effects. Over time and through diverse artistic interpretations, these variations have themselves been modified and metamorphosed into an even greater diversity of effects. Still, the resulting garments retain their connotative relationship to the original historical model.

One of the details that has come to denote the ancient silhouette is the cinching-in with a belt, the zōnē, that occurred above the natural waistline. In Napoleonic France, this "classical" waistline rose to a point directly under the bustline, even higher than the mid-ribcage level preferred by the ancients. This exaggeration, ubiquitous as a fashion during the neoclassical period from the 1790s through the 1810s, came to be called the Empire waist. Unlike the waistline of antiquity, which employed a cinch or belt, the Empire waist was structural with an almost vestigial bodice connected to a floor-length skirt by seaming.

While the chemise dress of the Empire period relied on pattern-cutting to establish the high neoclassical-style waistline, the fullness of ancient Greek apparel was controlled by the use of bindings and ties. Frequent depictions of double girdling on both the peplos and chiton suggest that the most common practice was to use one cinch functionally in order to pull in the waist and raise the hemline by hitching up the fabric to create a kolpos, or blouson. When a second binding was employed, it was worn over the blouson to establish a visible, decorative waistline. Over the centuries, artists and designers have used both double girdling and the blouson to imbue their creations with a relationship to this ancient practice.

Another zone of classical allusion has been the neckline. Antique representations of one-shouldered, breast-baring garments shown on goddesses and Amazons as a specific signifier of their mythic identity are the basis for the association of asymmetrical necklines with Hellenic attire.

Over the two millennia that separate us from their Græco-Roman ancestry, a small number of clothing types have come to represent the classical antique. But the many inventive and independent ancient variations in the method of wearing the peplos, chiton, and himation have also been transmitted. Even when at a considerable remove from a direct reference to specific ancient garment types and their manipulated forms, such details retain the ability to invoke a classical mode.

The harnessing of a chiton's sleeves seen in this Greek marble is often associated with Artemis. However, this figure's more substantial, slightly matronly form is the basis for an attribution of the sculpture's subject as Themis, goddess of custom and law. The artist sensitively rendered the surface of the wool himation and the linen chiton to indicate the individual characteristics of the two textiles. Themis is girded above her natural waist and a small distance below her bust. In later artistic representations of this classical preference for a slightly raised waistline, the cinching migrated upward until it was immediately under the breast in nineteenth-century neoclassical dress. Called the Empire waistline because of its association with the dress styles of the Napoleonic period, this high waist came to be another convention of classicizing fashion.

Greek. *Themis (Goddess of Custom and Law)*, marble, 2nd half of the 4th century B.C. The Metropolitan Museum of Art, Gift of Mrs. Frederick F. Thompson, 1903 (03.12.17). Photograph: Bruce White

With the French Revolution, the heavily boned and full-skirted silhouettes of traditional aristocratic attire gave way to the ideological preference for what the Revolutionaries took to be the form and substance of classical dress. During the Directoire and the Napoleonic Empire periods, sheer neoclassical styles based on high-waisted "Grecian" dress became the vogue. In this portrait, Madame Charles-Maurice de Talleyrand-Périgord's embrace of the antique is reflected in both her gown and the décor. Fashions of the period are known for their disclosure of the natural body. But while the stiffly boned corsets of the preceding *ancien régime* disappeared, a lighter version evolved, which was more cylindrical than the inverted cone shape of its predecessors. The new, more supple corsets commonly controlled the body through stiffened corded lines of quilting and the insertion of a center-front busk, a stiff stay of wood, metal, or whalebone. But the single transformation of the silhouette that has most come to characterize the fashions of the period was the raising of the waistline to directly below the bust. This portrait includes an additional classicizing detail: the draped fastening at the cap of the dress's oversleeve is an allusion to the button closures at the shoulderlines of the chiton.

Baron François-Pascal-Simon Gérard, French (1770–1837). *Madame Charles-Maurice de Talleyrand-Périgord, Princess de Bénévent (née Catherine Noele Worlée, later Madame George Francis Grand, 1762–1835)*, oil on unlined canvas, ca. 1808. The Metropolitan Museum of Art, Wrightsman Fund, 2002 (2002.31)

The combination of white mull, a thin and almost sheer cotton, with a cylindrical silhouette and a high Empire waistline comprises a potent evocation of classical dress. Although there are many images depicting the belting of chitons and peploi above the natural waistline, the raised waist was rarely positioned directly under the bust. This neoclassical mannerism abetted the illusion of the body as a dramatically linear and columnar form. Fashionable Directoire and Empire beauties, however, did not embrace the architectonic solidity of ancient caryatids. Instead, their classicism was aligned with an arcadian "naturalism" that rationalized the disclosure of the supple female form. Observers of the period frequently deplored the absence of modesty conveyed by a style that was predicated on the prominence and exposure of the breasts and on the barely veiled body. The women of ancient Greece, generally swathed in modesty, would have been startled by this promiscuous public display.

French. Two dresses, white mull, ca.1810. The Metropolitan Museum of Art, The Costume Institute. Left: Purchase: Gifts in memory of Elizabeth N. Lawrence, 1983 (1983.6.1); right: Rogers Fund, 1907 (TSR 07.146.5)

This 1937 drawing by Jean Cocteau depicts a gown by Alix, later known and remembered today as Madame Grès. The fabric falls in vertical folds similar to the lines of pleating seen in the *Charioteer of Delphi*, shown on page 12. However, Cocteau suggested another well-known artwork. The model reclines in the wanton posture of the famous early-second-century B.C. nude sculpture of a sleeping satyr known as *The Barberini Faun*. As seen in the image of the *Wounded Amazon* shown on page 110, the arm folded at the elbow and thrown back conveys not only sleep but also death. In both ancient works and the Cocteau drawing, the exposed vulnerability of the figure invites a voyeuristic gaze. Classical girdling was intended to control the fullness of the peplos and chiton. It was also used to draw up the garment's hem off the floor. The excess was bloused into a kolpos, obliterating the cinch. Often, a second, clearly visible overgirdle was worn below the bust. In this 1930s version of double girdling by Grès, there is no kolpos, and as a result, both bands are visible.

Black chiffon gathered and bound like a caryatid
by the hand of the sculptor Alix. Henri Bendel.

Jean

The designs of Miuccia Prada often subvert the conventional personae of women through irony, exaggeration, or recontexualization. In dealing with the potent transformative possibilities of dress, her interests focus on the iconography of female identity. In this advertising image, Prada, working with photographer Steven Meisel, mediated classicism through the glamorous 1930s style of the Hollywood portrait photographer George Hurrell. In a surprising coincidence, both dress and pose adumbrate the Cocteau drawing from the same period shown on page 97. That the Cocteau drawing and Grès gown are themselves reiterations of classical forms establishes the attenuated lineage of classical styles.

The ability of the simple conjuction of pleating and girdling to invoke the past is more unexpected in John Galliano's wild conflation of Nordic barbarians and 1930s-style Grecian goddesses, shown on the overleaf. Even the most discrete bits of classical dress—vestigial scraps of pleated cloth and irregular bindings of the midriff—can retain their iconographic power. Like Alexander McQueen and Tom Ford, Galliano has often shared the idealized beauty of classicism to achieve an aggressive feminist identity. The models stranded on a beach in this Steven Klein photograph have elements of Grecian style, and like participants in a mythic version of "Survivor," they exude a strong atavistic ferocity. The copy accompanying the photograph is an overwrought mix of references to reality television and allusions to the isles of Calypso and Circe that establishes a connection to the often lurid classicism encountered in Homer's *Odyssey*. It reads: "There's an orgy of exhibitionism, a voraciousness of voyeurism, Temptation Island. Hell hath no furies like the sinful silicone seductresses on the Fox Network."

Left: Prada, Italian (founded 1913). Dress, silk jersey, fall–winter 2002. Photograph of Amber Valletta by Steven Meisel courtesy of A+C Anthology.

Overleaf: Christian Dior Haute Couture, French (founded 1947), by John Galliano, British (born Gibraltar 1960). Six dresses, silk jersey and chiffon, spring–summer 2001. Group of models photographed by Steven Klein courtesy of *Vogue*

In this dress from 1950, Claire McCardell used two layers of pleated nylon chiffon, café au lait over pale beige, to create a neoclassical gown of smoky ethereality. The narrow self-cording that creates a spaghetti-strap neckline and forms the cinched midriff is a signature element of McCardell's work. This cording is stitched to the gown in an Empire waistline with its ends free to tie according to personal preference. As a student in the Parsons design program in France, McCardell was exposed to the work of Madame Grès and Madeleine Vionnet, purchasing any examples of their Grecian styles that appeared at the Paris flea markets to disassemble and study. The imprint of these two classicizing designers of the haute couture are seen in this gown. However, as a designer of ready-to-wear, McCardell was precluded from employing many of the technical refinements available in the couture. Her genius was in her ability to retain the effects of that elite practice despite the limitations of the manufacturing process.

Similarly, after working in Paris for Christian Lacroix and John Galliano at Christian Dior, Lars Nilsson introduced the sophisticated approaches of the haute couture to Bill Blass, a design house known for its all-American sensibility. In the dress shown on the overleaf, Nilsson created a classical effect through the design's conjunction of nudity, simplicity, drapery, and, most importantly, a double-girdled waist, here marked by dark bugle-beaded bands. The classical midriff treatment is interpreted in a way that introduces an element of contemporaneity to the venerable form. In Nilsson's design, the midriff bands do not meet at center-front but instead terminate in skewed, sharply angled ends. This detail adds a provocative deconstructivist quality to a design of otherwise old school, Bill Blass suavity.

Right: Claire McCardell, American (1905–1958), Empire dress, beige pleated nylon chiffon, 1950. Lent by The Museum at The Fashion Institute of Technology, New York, Gift of Mr. and Mrs. Adrian McCardell (72.61.181). Overleaf: Bill Blass Ltd., American (founded 1970), by Lars Nilsson, Swedish (born 1966). Evening dress, silver silk, resort 2002. Photograph of Christy Turlington by Steven Klein courtesy of *Vogue*

The wish for an accurate rendering of classical drapery and dress was increasingly pronounced by the mid-eighteenth century. This impulse was abetted by the interest surrounding earlier excavations of Pompeii and Herculaneum, the proliferation and wide dissemination of prints describing important classical works, and the writings of, among others, Johann Joachim Winkelmann, who used classical, specifically Greek artworks to substantiate his belief in the unsurpassed culture of ancient Greece. However, it was in the last decades of the eighteenth century and the beginning of the nineteenth century, when an association to the Greek polis was made to post-French Revolutionary culture, that the desire for an historical veracity of dress in art and fashion reached an apogee. For example, Thomas Hope's *Costumes of the Greeks and Romans*, first published in 1812, was an attempt to compile a patternbook of costume types. Its influence and inaccuracies extended into representations of classical dress in the fine arts and fashion. Often, artists of grand subjects and history paintings resorted to their own replication of classical dress, draping actual garments based on sculptural and painted examples. In the process, subtle modifications of the antique prototypes emerged. With its double girdling, Jean-Auguste-Dominique Ingres' chiton shown here has Hellenic precedent. But his depiction of the garment's sideseam, stitched only to the hip and leaving the right leg bare, is an anachronistic conceit.

Examples of double girdling of the chiton, with a visible overgirdle placed high and a lower undergirdle with full kolpos, appear in ancient Hellenic dress. This contemporary reprise of the style by Stéphane Rolland, designer for the House of Jean-Louis Scherrer, is modified to expose more of the wearer's body. Unlike a true chiton, the gown is constructed of three, rather than two panels of fabric. Two short lengths of crepe form a halter front that extends into a deep-plunging décolletage. A seam from the center waist forms the mini-length front. One longer panel attached from the waist at either sideseam extends into a long train. While some of the fabric has been cut away to create the arc of the skirt's hem, the Rolland design, like its classical predecessor, is developed primarily through the draping and seaming together of fabric rather than the shaping of pattern pieces.

House of Jean-Louis Scherrer, French (founded 1962), by Stéphane Rolland, French (born 1966). Evening gown, brown silk crepe, spring–summer 2002.
Courtesy of the House of Jean-Louis Scherrer

In ancient Hellenic representations of the Amazons, and in some instances of Artemis or other goddesses, the chiton was shown with one breast bared, a fashion called exomis. Through such examples as this statue of a wounded Amazon in an unfastened chiton, the one-shouldered neckline has come to be associated with classical dress.

In his depiction of an allegory of music as a classicized figure, shown on the overleaf, the seventeenth-century Baroque artist Laurent de la Hyre deliberately rendered the voluminous drapery to expose one breast. The details of dress are both studiously historical and inventively fictive. The button-closing sleeve treatment approximates the shoulder and sleeve closures of the chiton. But the red himation is gathered in folds, suggesting an excess of fullness beyond that of any Greek precedent. At the same time, the girdling strap anchors a small, narrow, and tightly twisted white scarf that is not typical of ancient dress. In this last instance, the scarf is a formal device of the painter, framing the left breast and underscoring its exposure— and the allusion to antique practice.

In this striking photograph by Richard Avedon, Sunny Harnett, a celebrated model of the day, wears a one-shouldered white silk jersey gown by Madame Grès. Unlike post-classical artistic citations of undone chitons, with their angled breast-exposing drape, many fashion designers have adopted the asymmetry of the neckline, while retreating from the full exposure of the breast. Gres' approach to fashion, as evidenced by her body-skimming designs of the 1930s, could not have been more different from Christian Dior's 1947 "New Look," which revived a wasp-waisted silhouette not seen since the end of the nineteenth century. However, even Grès, whose signature medium was a supple silk jersey, embraced the fashion for a structured underbodice introduced by Dior's hour-glass style. In doing so, she was able to create pieces of increasingly complex drapery and pleating by tacking her difficult medium onto the rigid form of the shaping underbodice. Her lacing of a gold lamé ribbon, which articulates the separate, vertically draped panels that run unbroken from neckline to hem, alludes to the girdling and quiver straps seen in classical renderings of Artemis.

The one-shouldered gown appeared in many of Halston's collections. He was especially interested in the bias-spiraling of fabric over the body. His most popular designs were often repeated in a variety of luxurious fabrics—silk chiffons, crepes, jerseys, hammered satin, and even cashmere knits. Halston rarely discussed the actual technical aspects of his work. On close examination, however, the apparent simplicity of his designs is extraordinary in its minimalist resolution. His teal gown, shown at left on the overleaf, extends into a wrap, as if himation and chiton were merged. His purple gown, at right on the overleaf, while not strictly one-shouldered, evolved from the pattern pieces of his earlier gowns with asymmetrical necklines. Although modest in its coverage of the body, its fissured and angled neckline and tentative anchoring on the right shoulder convey a potential for nudity and allude to the classical Greek fashion of anchoring the himation at the shoulder to fall down one side.

Left: Madame Grès, French (1903–1993). Evening gown, white silk jersey, 1954. Photograph of Sunny Harnett for *Harper's Bazaar* by Richard Avedon, American (born 1923), gelatin silver print, 1954. Courtesy of Richard Avedon Studio. Overleaf: Halston (Roy Halston Frowick), American (1932–1990). Left: Evening gown, iridescent teal and black silk chiffon, 1970s. The Metropolitan Museum of Art, The Costume Institute, Purchase: Janet A. Sloane Gift Fund, 1994 (1994.414.6). Right: Evening gown, purple silk chiffon, 1977. Courtesy of Rosina Rucci

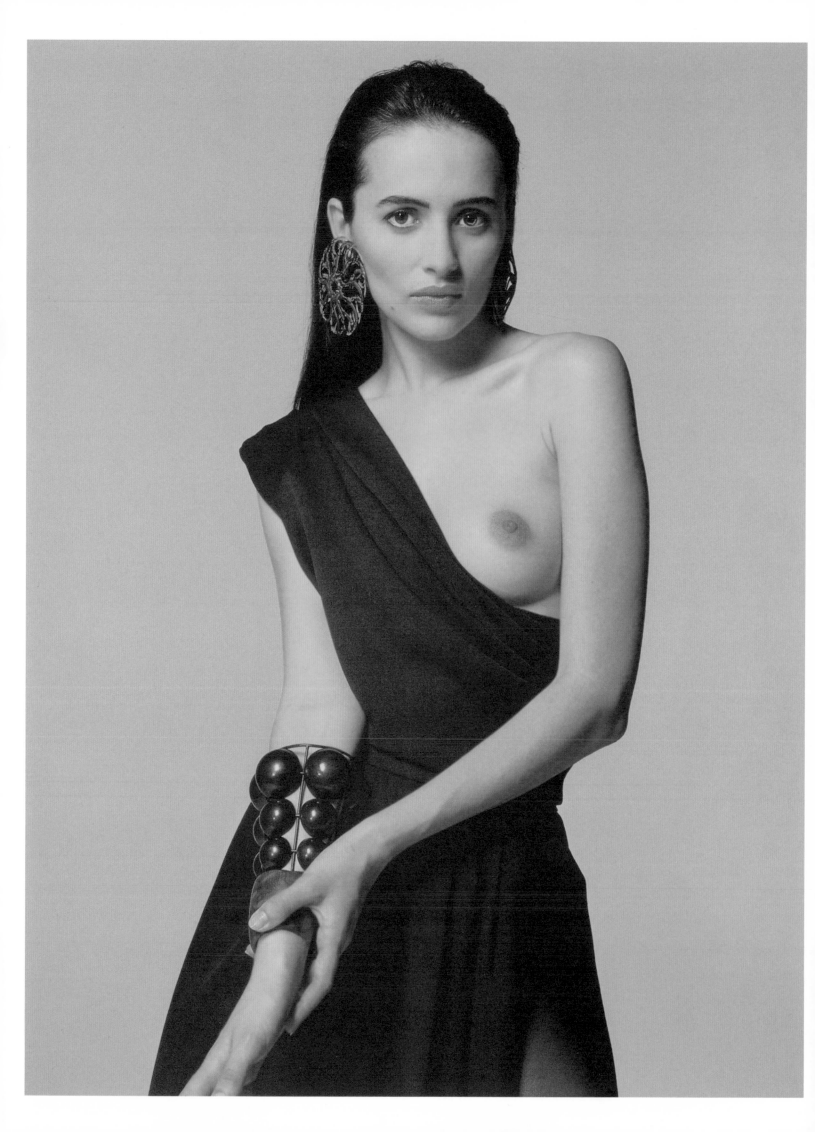

Yves Saint Laurent was at the pinnacle of the haute couture upon his emergence as the new head of the Maison Dior at the untimely death of Christian Dior in 1957, until the unexpected closure of Yves Saint Laurent Haute Couture in 2002. In his long career, Saint Laurent established, more than any of his contemporaries, an extraordinary repertoire of styles synonymous with his house. Whether inspired by art, foreign cultures, the street, or the evocative eras of the past, his romantic imagination consistently infused the poetic into works of elegant modernity. In his spring–summer 1990 collection, Saint Laurent revisited his interest in the softly draped, one-shoulder gown. It provoked some controversy, for the phalanx of models in these neoclassical dresses appeared with their left breasts boldly exposed. However, with his cool aestheticism, even the potentially sensational display of the female breast was mediated by a classical naturalism. Like Madame Grès who preferred boldly atavistic jewelry with her Grecian gowns, Saint Laurent chose to accessorize his gown with sculptural jewelry of an archaic simplicity. In William Laxton's photograph, the juxtaposition of the classical lines of the gown and the barbaric boldness of the jewelry suggests both a Homeric sorceress and the Amazons described by Herodotus.

Yves Saint Laurent Rive Gauche, French (founded 1966). Evening dress, brown silk crepe, spring–summer 1990. Photograph: William Laxton courtesy of *Vogue Paris*

Clements Ribeiro is the partnership of husband and wife Inacio Ribeiro and
Suzanne Clements. The couple are graduates of graduates of St. Martins, the
design program that has been the training ground for many of the most
influential designers of the last decade. Both their designs and the thematic
presentations of their work are characterized by an imaginative mix of
narrative allusions and materials. In the design shown here, they played with
classical imagery perceived through the lens of a 1950s Hollywood epic. With
characteristic subversive intention and wit, they strapped a diaphanous
chiffon chiton with a thick metal-eyeleted belt, creating a dress appropriate
for a contemporary Amazon. In the photograph, the stylist has exaggerated
the martial quality of the dress by pairing it with black leather motorcycle
boots, a gender-crossing and anachronistic, hence modernizing, element.

Far left is a deceptively simple evening dress designed in 1962 by Cristobal Balenciaga. The Spanish-born couturier is considered the supreme architect of twentieth-century fashion. Remembered primarily for his virtuosity as a tailor and for his use of fabrics with a stiffer or more structured "hand," Balenciaga generally sheathed the body in a self-supporting armature of cloth. In this extraordinary example, he manipulated a luxurious silk satin on the bias. With the exception of the back scarf panel, this gown is cut-in-one, like a piece of soft origami. The fabric is seamed at a diagonal in the back but lacks any darts for fit. In its economy, Balenciaga's gown is like the single panel constructions of the peplos, but its technical sophistication is unlike that of any preceding form. Near left is a recent design by Giorgio Armani. Like Balenciaga, Armani created a form of tailoring reliant on the structure and draping characteristics of the cloth rather than on interfacings and padding of traditional tailored garments. In the instance of draped eveningwear, however, Armani could not be more distinct in his interests and approaches. This one-shouldered "gown" is actually a jumpsuit, ending in tightly fitted Asian dhoti-style ankle cuffs that gather the fabric up into a soft harem hem. The half-bow at the shoulder is a separate scarf that can be arranged to the taste of the wearer.

Left: Cristobal Balenciaga, French (born Spain 1895–1972). Evening gown, light-blue silk satin, 1965. The Metropolitan Museum of Art, The Costume Institute, Gift of Anonymous (1973.139). Right: Giorgio Armani, Italian (born 1934). Jumpsuit, gray silk satin, fall–winter 2002. Courtesy of Giorgio Armani

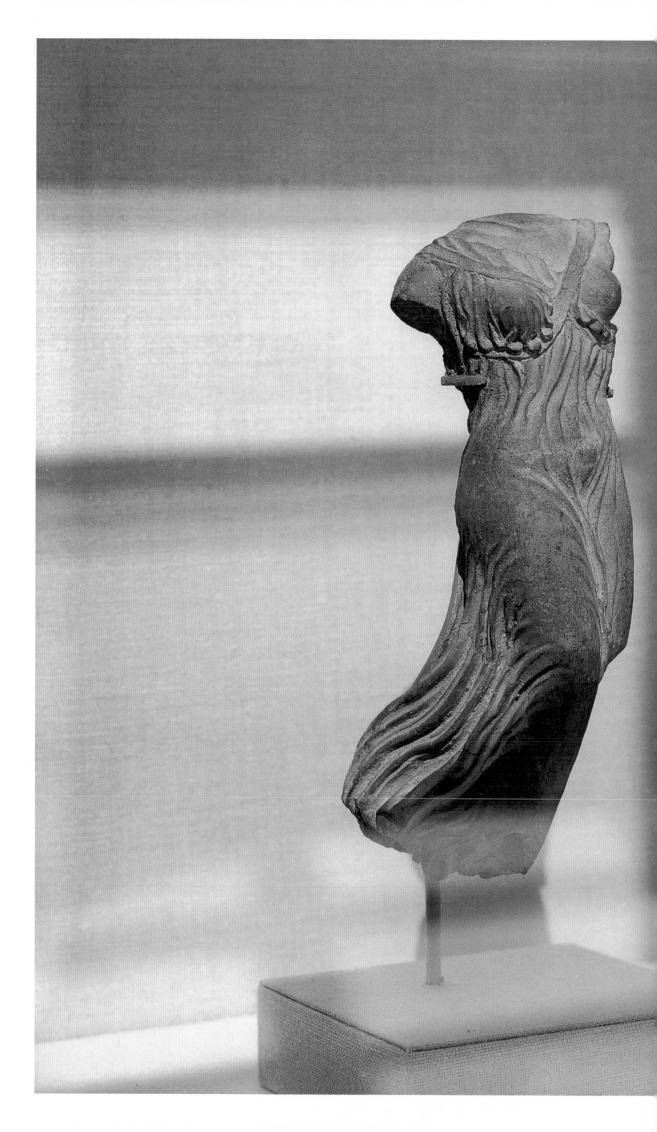

The use of harnesses to pull in the full volume of the chiton and peplos is well represented in classical Greek art. In most instances, shoulder harnesses intended to rein in the sleeves crisscross in the back and loop in a raglan line at the front. However, examples exist in which the crossing of the harness forms an X in front, separating the breasts as in the Nike on the preceding pages, and perhaps more famously in the fragment of Selene, goddess of the moon, from the pediment of the Parthenon. Despite the relative infrequency of its depiction, this detail has been embraced widely by later artists and designers. In the early-nineteenth-century portrait on the facing page, Elizabeth Patterson Bonaparte, the first wife of Jerome Bonaparte, brother of Napoleon, wears a fashionable dress with thin gold braid as a purely decorative replication of the classical harness. A small gilt button at either shoulder further substantiates the antique model, referencing the buttons that formed a chiton's sleeves and the use of fibulae that fixed the shoulders of a peplos.

Preceding pages: Greek. *The Personification of Nike*, terracotta statuette, late 5th century B.C. The Metropolitan Museum of Art, Rogers Fund, 1907 (07.286.23). Photograph: Bruce Schwarz. Facing page: Franciscus Josephus Kinson, French (1770–1839). *Elizabeth Patterson Bonaparte (1785–1879)*, oil on canvas, 1817. The Maryland Historical Society, Baltimore, Maryland

Mariano Fortuny's pleated evening dresses, often accompanied by coordinated cloaks, shawls, or jackets, were originally designed to be worn as tea gowns. That is, they were intended as "undress" to be worn at home for informal entertaining. By the 1920s, however, as styles and mores evolved, their jewel-like colors and body-conforming sensuality made them seductive evening attire. Worn outside the home by the fashionably adventurous—the actresses Lillian and Dorothy Gish, and Natasha Rambova, the wife of Rudolf Valentino, are notable American examples— the gowns were available in a variety of styles. This particular example is a relatively rare model—a simple chiton with Venetian glass buttons fastening the topline of the fitted sleeves and a cross harness. As in the dress worn by Elizabeth Bonaparte, shown on page 126, the harness is fixed and purely decorative. Fortuny, however, is known to have made functional versions with cording subject to manipulation and adjustment.

Mariano Fortuny, Italian (born Spain 1871–1949). Evening gown, pale-pink pleated silk with pink silk cord and glass beads, 1920s. The Metropolitan Museum of Art, The Costume Institute, Gift of Estate of Lillian Gish, 1995 (1995.28.6a)

French designer Maggy Rouff began her career with simple, sportswear-inflected designs. She was known for her deft use of feminine dressmaker's details such as shirring, attached scarves, bias flounces, and ruffles. In this example, the horizontal gathering at the bodice of the gown is generated by a Grecian-style harness. Although the drapery is fixed, a lamé ribbon can adjust the tension at the waist. The designer's allusion to the antique is reinforced by the photographer George Hoyningen-Huene's positioning of the model next to an archaistic Greek sculptural fragment with swallowtail folds. Numerous references to the antique appear in Hoyningen-Huene's fashion work. Often, the evocations of classical style were made by architectural elements, such as a column or pedestal, decorative elements as in a piece of furniture, artworks such as an urn, or as in this example, a sculpture. These props, together with the simple, generally fluidly draped gowns they framed, established a mood of serene, if self-consciously staged classicism. The aristocratic Russian émigré's abiding interest in the Hellenic world culminated in the 1943 publication of his book titled *Hellas: A Tribute to Classical Greece*.

Maggy Rouff, French (1896–1971). Evening gown, white, silver and gold lamé, 1939. Photograph by George Hoyningen-Huene courtesy of *Harper's Bazaar*

PYGMALION'S GALATEA: ART TO LIFE

The Roman poet Ovid recounted an ancient myth in which Pygmalion, a sculptor disenchanted by mortal women, creates an image of feminine perfection. When he becomes enthralled with his own sculpted ideal, Venus—the Greek Aphrodite—responds to his prayers and brings the statue to life as Galatea.

Through the centuries, art and fashion have achieved their own transformations, introducing in the process new qualities not present in the original garments. Even in the most naturalistic representation of Hellenic dress, subjective and proscribed stylistic qualities are inevitably introduced. In depicting details of the distinctive modes of ancient Greek attire, subsequent artists and designers have changed, as much as preserved, the actual qualities of ancient garb. Among the stylizations that have most influenced fashion designers is wet-drapery, a term used by art historians to describe cloth that appears to cling to the body in animated folds while it reveals the contours of the form beneath. This sculptural characteristic—evidenced in figures from the classical and Hellenistic periods—has emerged in fashion as a signifier of classicizing intent. From the nineteenth century to the present, designers have utilized a variety of techniques and materials to replicate its effects in cloth.

In certain artistic renderings from antiquity, textiles appear fragile, and even ephemeral, qualities that are substantiated in ancient literary texts. Such gossamer robes, shawls, and veilings became one of the antique's most potent associations for fashion, as exemplified by the popular use of light mull, a sheer cotton fabric of the Empire period, and also of tulle and chiffon. The classicizing effect is further underscored if the fabric is white, since there has been a longstanding convention that ancient Grecian styles should be achromatic. This misconception, thought to derive from the faded and abraded surfaces of originally polychromed Greek statuary and architecture, continues to this day in fashion.

Drapery of the classical and Hellenistic periods of Greek art sometimes appears purely as a foil for nudity, clinging and spiraling around the body. Often, this effect occurs in response to compositional requirements rather than to any natural phenomenon or dressing practice. Such animated drapery frequently takes on a more schematic form, with fluted edges regularized into a rhythmic pattern of handkerchief-pointed "swallowtail" folds, a characteristic that has inspired fashion designers in the twentieth century.

In Greek art, fabrics are rendered with the texture of both regular folds and irregular pleating. Such differentiated representations have also found expression in fashion design. By employing a variety of techniques, designers as disparate as Mariano Fortuny, Madeleine Vionnet, Madame Grès, Mary McFadden, and Norma Kamali have achieved effects redolent of the stylized characteristics of cloth seen in the art of ancient Greece.

In the Louvre's famous Hellenistic marble *Victory of Samothrace*, the winged goddess of victory, or Nike, seems to confront a gust of wind. Her peplos cleaves so closely to her body that her breasts and navel are fully disclosed. This rendering of wet-drapery hyperbolizes the flowing folds of actual dress, and suggests a body-revealing sheerness possible only with the most finely woven cloth. In addition, her himation, twisted into a narrow coil, is shown spiraling around her right hip and blowing against her legs by the force of the wind. The himation's suspension on the Nike's hip anticipates a later convention in fashion, in which self-animated loops of drapery attach to the body without the naturalistic rationalization of the buffeting gust seen here. The goddess was undoubtedly depicted with her right arm held high. It is thought that she was placed in the sanctuary of the Great Gods on the Isle of Samothrace, as if on the prow of a ship, to celebrate a success at sea, a victory by the Rhodians around 200 B.C.

Greek. *Victory of Samothrace*, marble, ca. 190 B.C. Paris, Musée du Louvre. Photograph © Réunion des Musées Nationaux/Art Resource, NY

Like the *Victory of Samothrace*, this Venus by the nineteenth-century British Pre-Raphaelite artist Edward Burne-Jones is dressed in rippling fabric that reveals the attributes of her physical beauty beneath. All the figures in this painting wear garments that neither conform to the details of classical dress nor, in fact, to any replicable garment. Instead, their clinging folds and twisted bindings are purely subject to the artist's imagination and signature style. Despite their stylization, however, it is through their allusion to the wet-drapery of antique models that the gowns convey their classicism. Unlike their more academic colleagues, the Pre-Raphaelites appear to have been less conscientious in the accuracy of their costuming of classical and medieval themes. In contrast to their renderings of Biblical subjects, in which Near and Middle Eastern vernacular garments were cited as appropriate references, the mythic world of the Greek pantheon seems to have provided them with opportunities for wildly imaginative license.

Edward Burne-Jones, British (1833–1896). *The Mirror of Venus* (detail), oil on canvas, 1873–1877. Photograph © Art Resource, NY

The design house Liberty & Company was known for its "artistic" dresses, with romantic and artisanal medieval effects, or faintly exotic and orientalizing motifs and silhouettes. This evening dress is particularly rare and unusual in that it fully incorporates what were viewed as classical elements of the period. The asymmetrical bodice with chiton sleeves alludes to the wearing of a himation anchored at one shoulder. Likewise, the two bow-knots replace the fibulae that would have held together an ancient peplos. But the strongest classicizing detail of the gown is in its densely gathered silk, a technique that conjures the wet-drapery of classical statuary. While the gown's internal structure, with a wasp-waisted corset and bell-shaped underskirt, conforms to the fashionable hourglass silhouette of the period, its surface is intended to replicate the articulated folds that characterize classical renderings of drapery. This softly gathered surface would also have conveyed a tantalizing "naturalism." The consequence is an impression of the female body as less confined by the rectitude of a precise and controlled tailoring.

Attributed to Liberty of London, British (founded 1875). Evening gown, yellow China silk, 1880s. The Metropolitan Museum of Art, The Costume Institute, Purchase: Gifts from Various Donors Fund, 1985 (1985.155)

Like the 1880s dress by Liberty on the previous pages, this post-New Look evening gown by Pierre Balmain achieves its elaborately gathered surface by loosely tacking a supple fabric onto a rigid body-shaping support. In this case, the fabric is silk georgette, a chiffon with elastic high-twist threads. Balmain employed chiffon as a medium for fluid effects, as Madame Grès used the light-ply jersey she favored in her classicizing designs. It is as if wet-drapery, the stylistic mannerism of ancient Greek sculptors, has been replicated in cloth. A bow at the small of the back marks the terminus of the garment's trompe l'oeil waist closure. Like the shoulder bows of the Liberty dress, the bow-knot is a decorative anachronism, alluding to the waist tie of classical girdling and also to the Renaissance convention of knotting as a denotation of classical-garment construction. A gown imbued with a classical narrative would have fulfilled perfectly the requirements of the Balmain client. The house was noted for designs for the *jolie madame*— pretty and elegant dressing for the woman who sought to be à la mode without controversy.

Pierre Balmain, French (1914–1982). Evening gown (two views), pale-blue silk georgette, 1957. Courtesy of Sandy Schreier

By the twentieth century, the pleating and the girdled midriff of this halter gown were well-established references to classicism. But in this dress, Edward Molyneux introduced a subtle new detail to frozen wet-drapery by replicating the fluted neckline seen on many Greek and Roman statues. As in Hellenistic sculptures, Molyneux fanned open the pleats of his gown's deep décolleté neckline. But like most pleated gowns of the post-World-War-II era, these folds are carefully controlled and secured by loose stitches to a structured, though in this instance flexible, underbodice. The modernist movement's affinity with classicism is evidenced in fashion from the beginning of the twentieth century onward. Here, the designer manipulated an experimental fabric into forms evocative of the antique. However specifically situated classical dress was to its own time, references to Hellenic styles have been freed from fashion's chronology by a sense of the timelessness of the ideals of beauty they evoke. In choosing to cite the past while also experimenting with a fabric of the future, Molyneux aligned himself with designers for theater and film, who costume imagined utopias past and future with the draped styles of the ancients.

Edward Molyneux, French (born Britain 1891–1974). Evening gown, mauve acetate satin-backed crepe, 1949. The Metropolitan Museum of Art, The Costume Institute, Gift of A. M. Tenney Associates, Inc. and Tennessee Eastman Corporation, 1949 (CI 50.21.12)

Issey Miyake has established a career based on innovations of cut, textile development, and more recently, adventurous artistic collaborations. In this dress, he explored a recurrent theme in his work: the transformation of two-dimensional cloth into three-dimensional clothing, without relying on Western tailoring conventions. Miyake accomplished the fit of the gown by shaping and manipulating the liquid drape of the bodice by hand on fiberglass mannequins. He soaked the length of synthetic jersey with a liquid polymer in the areas where he desired a fixed wet-drapery effect. When the polymer hardened, the cuirasse-like bodice could be lifted off the mannequin. With essentially one continuous length of cloth that spiraled around the body, Miyake created a garment without cutting or stitching. The detail seen here focuses on the polymer-stiffened zone of the bodice, but the similarity to classical drapery is also evident in the untreated lengths of cloth that extend from the shoulder and waist to form the gown's soft, fluid back and skirt.

Issey Miyake, Japanese (born 1938). "Waterfall Body" dress (detail), acetate and polyurethane resin, fall–winter 1984. Photograph by Tsutomu Wakatsuki courtesy of Miyake Design Studio

Tom Ford's historicizing methodology has been evident from his first collection as designer for Gucci. His initial focus was on the relatively recent past, the 1970s. In later collections, for both Gucci and Yves Saint Laurent Rive Gauche, Ford has alluded to the classical past. Rather than the knowing but immediately accessible citations that characterized his early work, Ford has begun to layer and synthesize his allusions. This tightly pleated gown references the effects of Madame Grès, who also introduced fissures and openings to the body in her garments. However, here the chiffon is handled roughly, the pleats are irregular, and the edges of the cloth are pulled and frayed. Unlike the cool perfection associated with classicism in the past, Ford's design projects an antique of artisanal beauty, a Hellenism poised between the crude and the refined. Working with a repertoire of leitmotifs established by Saint Laurent, Ford has been oblique in his quotations of the company's rich heritage. Saint Laurent's collections often included a number of fluid gowns alluding to the antique, but the sensuality of his work was always mediated by the chill of his intellect, distanced from any hint of vulgarity or the profane. Ford's effects are deliberately visceral and explicitly sexual, perhaps reflecting a belief that there can be an excess of refinement, and that calculated imperfection might introduce a seductive approachability.

Yves Saint Laurent Rive Gauche, French (founded 1966) by Tom Ford, American (born 1961). Evening dress, fuchsia silk chiffon, resort 2002. Photograph of actress Julianne Moore © Michael Thompson

A postmodernist mix is apparent in many of John Galliano's designs, often in dramatically discordant juxtaposition. However, in this example, he has reiterated analogous effects by superimposing an airbrushed image of drapery on a gown that is itself discreetly draped. Among the many themes that emerge in Galliano's work, neoclassicism and the fashions of the 1930s are perhaps his most favored and revisited. For his own signature label, he presented a spring–summer 1986 collection, "Les Incroyables," based on the *Incroyables* and *Merveilleuse*, who at the end-of-the-eighteenth-century Directoire era embraced an exaggerated neoclassical style. Galliano's spring–summer 1989 collection focused on a Europe-between-the-world-wars vision of bias dresses with a sultry decadence. In this example, the trompe l'oeil folds of the painted himation over the body-glove fit of a 1930s-style sheath suggest a conflation of ideas originating in these earlier collections. Additionally, Galliano injected an allusion to Elsa Schiaparelli's surrealist-inspired collections by presenting this gown on the runway, framed by torn paper with the model's head covered in thick chalk-white makeup. Crowned by unruly ivy vines that tumbled down her neck, the white face gave the model the uncanny appearance of an animated garden sculpture.

Christian Dior Haute Couture, French (founded 1947), by John Galliano, British (born Gibralter 1960). Evening gown, taupe hand-printed silk crepe, spring–summer 1999. Courtesy Mrs. Veronica Hearst

Through the twentieth century, classical dress accrued a number of associations, some more and others less historically apt. Certain of them—body consciousness, simple untailored construction, deeply draped folds, insubstantial and unlined materials—were assimilated into the designs of "undress," in the form of "Grecian" tea gowns, peignoirs, and nightgowns. Shown here is intimate apparel designer Lucie Ann's chartreuse chiffon peignoir, worn by the actress Julie Newmar, who is best remembered today for her 1966 appearances as Catwoman on ABC's high-camp series "Batman." Lucie Ann's sheer peignoir is constructed of two simple rectangles like those of a chiton, but knotted at the shoulders. While the Greeks do not appear to have used this method as a garment construction detail, it has come to characterize an antique form because of its technical simplicity.

Lucie Ann, American (founded ca. 1960). Peignoir, chartreuse silk chiffon, 1962. Photograph of Julie Newmar by Bert Stern courtesy of *Vogue*

Christian Lacroix made a flamboyant entry into the world of haute couture as the designer for Patou in 1981. His imaginative designs were inspired by the extravagance that characterized the theatrical hedonism of the Moulin Rouge can-can dancers in late-nineteenth-century Montmartre. This chaste gown contradicts his reputation as the master collagist of the French métièrs—the artisanal trades of textile, feather, silk flower, embroidery, leather, and passementerie that support the exquisite effects of the haute couture. Lacroix's shirring and gathering of silk tulle into folds suggest a merging of wet-drapery effects with the neoclassical fashions of the late-eighteenth-century Directoire period. While tulle is often thought of as the nylon or starched cotton netting in the stiff layers of a crinoline underskirt, here it is made of a fine and supple unstarched silk. Despite its ability to hold Lacroix's carefully draped relief, silk tulle also retains its wafting and flowing qualities, contributing to the romantic ethereality of this diaphanous white gown.

Christian Lacroix, French (born 1951). Evening gown, white tulle, spring–summer 1998. Photograph by Thomas Schenk courtesy of *L'Officiel*

Dolce & Gabbana's spring–summer 2003 presentation culminated in a rush of "classical" maidens. Dressed in gossamer tops with sandals appropriate for the hunt, they recalled the Greek goddess Artemis. The models raced down the runway at a pace intended both to animate their light garments and to draw them against their bodies. Recalling the wet-drapery of the *Victory of Samothrace*, the gathered and blousoned white chiffon ensembles provided a dramatically agitated surface of folds and a sensual disclosure of the body beneath. The designers, Domenico Dolce and Stefano Gabbana, are famous for their knowing manipulations of sexual stereotypes and their provocative mixing of high and low cultural references. They subvert culturally bound expectations of male and female, even as they embrace and exaggerate familiar attributes of gender. In this example, ethereal feminine effects were accompanied by an element of almost discordant masculinity: calf-height, studded black leather sandals. By merging disjunctive elements from the dress of woodland nymphs and Homeric heroes, these designers, perhaps serendipitously, suggested the ambiguous allure of Artemis, whose chiton was raised like a man's to free her legs and whose sandals were strapped securely to endure the rigors of the chase.

Dolce & Gabbana, Italian (founded 1982). Evening dress, white silk chiffon, spring–summer 2003. Courtesy of Dolce & Gabbana

Designers in the twentieth century have been inspired by and have replicated the stop-action quality of drapery seen in classical sculpture. The precariously poised himation represented as a wide swath of cloth around the loins of the *Venus de Milo*, for example, suggests she is caught in freeze-frame. Other versions of Venus, Aphrodite to the Greeks, depict her with similar variations of drapery, slung low around her hips and rendered in the artistic stylization of cloth in sweeping animation rather than in motionless fall. In addition, the survival of sculptural fragments with small remnants of costume attached also contribute to the idea of classical drapery as discrete and vivified forms. When the effect of animated, or even agitated, drapery has been cited by fashion designers, the fabric is paradoxically fixed into place to convey the sense of cloth in movement seen in antique artworks.

Greek. *Venus de Milo*, marble, ca. 100 B.C. Paris, Musée du Louvre. Photograph © Réunion des Musées Nationaux/Art Resource, NY

Compared to some of Jean Paul Gaultier's fashions of hyperbolic gender exaggeration and transgression, this tank dress with a photo-print is relatively subdued. However, when seen on a real woman, the superimposition of a half-naked statue's anatomy over the body is unexpectedly lurid. The designer carried the joke to the verso of the dress, which depicts the statue's back view. Gaultier's fashion provocations are invariably leavened with humor, even when he is inspired by Hellenic art. In one of his more controversial applications of the photo-print process, he used fabric that depicts couples in exotic and acrobatic sexual play, in the manner of ancient Greek Attic red-figure vase painting. Gaultier's classical influences have not been restricted to womenswear. In his menswear, the antique appears in the form of fantasies of faintly threatening, hyper-mesomorphic gladiators, like those in the work of contemporary artist Tom of Finland.

Jean Paul Gaultier, French (born 1952). Evening gown, white silk with black photo-print of *Venus of Arles* sculpture, spring–summer 1999. Courtesy of Sandy Schreier

In this haute couture gown by John Galliano for Christian Dior, the classical allusions are its body-wrapping construction and the appearance of animated bits of drapery that attach to it like the himations and scarves seen on classical nude images. Gold lamé, sunburst pleating, and the trapunto, or channel stitched, quilting seen here all had a period of popularity in the 1930s. Together with the gown's asymmetrical draping, these details inspire an inevitable association with the revealing bias styles that predated World War II. The trapunto epaulets are shifted, and in one instance displaced to the small of the back. They create the effect of stiffened drapery caught around an essentially simple body-cleaving gown. Pleated insertions appear to be unstitched and reassembled into an asymmetrical, spiraling swallowtail train. Worn by recent Golden Globe award winner Nicole Kidman to the Academy Awards in 2000, the gown established a connection with the glamorous tradition of Hollywood screen stars of the 1930s, as well as with the gilded contours of the Oscar itself. Galliano has created a number of evening gowns that have taken apart vintage styles and reworked and reassembled them into surprising and technically audacious configurations. In this instance, his deconstructed Deco-style classicism is the result of a process that can be termed auto-cannibalism. Originally, his gown was shown on the runway in white silk. Galliano took that gown, an homage to the great couture traditions of the 1930s, reconfigured it into this style, and then rendered it in gold for Ms. Kidman.

Christian Dior Haute Couture, French (founded 1947), by John Galliano, British (born Gibraltar 1960). Dress, gold metallic thread and wool lamé, spring–summer 2000. Courtesy of Nicole Kidman

In this photograph by Michelangelo Di Battista, showing a bathing suit by La Perla, a backlit stairway leads to a gated exit. Chinese characters appear on the wall, framing the scene on the right. Such compositional components hardly support a classical narrative. Still, the potency of certain elements derived from classical statuary conveys a connection to the antique that is powerful enough to disrupt the more apparent meanings intended by the photographer and stylist. In this spandex bathing suit, the white material, wrapped construction, and most importantly, the drapery falling at the left breast in a swallowtail fold all connote the classical. The model's blonde hair is styled in a wave made famous by Veronica Lake, the sultry Hollywood movie star of the early 1940s. The accessorizing of the bathing suit with high-heeled gilt sandals situates this "goddess" in the louche world of film noir. The unavoidable suggestion is that she is a contemporary hetæra, or beauty for hire, thus subverting the popular notion that classical deification is equivalent with unattainability.

La Perla, Italian (founded 1954). Bathing suit, white spandex, spring–summer 2002. Photograph by Michelangelo Di Battista courtesy of La Perla

This red-figure Greek vase depicts Poseidon, the god of the sea and the brother of Zeus and Hades, pursuing Amymone, the daughter of the king of Argos. Amymone's costume shows the neatly fluted patterning of the swallowtail fold, a classical convention in the rendering of drapery, particularly of fabric falling on the bias and terminating in the pointed corner of a garment. At the terminus of such fluting is a zig-zag hemline called the handkerchief hem. The stylized linearity represented here also occurs in sculpture of the sixth century B.C., the so-called archaic period. In fashion design, the swallowtail fold and handkerchief hem appear commonly as components intended to evoke the ideal beauty of the antique. As a design element, the swallowtail relies on the intrinsic qualities of cloth, and is free of any technical complication other than the simple release of fabric into a free drape. The swallowtail fold and the handkerchief hem conform to the modernist notion that classical forms are the result of only the most minimal dressmaking intervention.

Greek (Attic). *Poseidon Pursuing Amymone*, terracotta, ca. 440 B.C. The Metropolitan Museum of Art, Rogers Fund, 1917 (17.230.35)

Mariano Fortuny created a number of variations of his pleated silk gowns. In this model, he combined elements of the classical chiton and the peplos. A "tunic" is attached along its neckline to a long sleeveless underdress, suggesting the apoptygma of the classical peplos. This effect is further emphasized by the handkerchief points at either hip, which would have been seen on the sides of an authentic apoptygma. In the ancient Grecian peplos, the arm openings were positioned along the neckline edge rather than the sideseam edges. This resulted in a dipping hemline at either side of the garment when worn. Fortuny took this structural attribute and achieved the similar, purely decorative effect by cutting away at the tunic's front and back hem. Further, he interpreted the buttoned or pinned closings characteristic of a chiton's shoulder seams by connecting the topline seam of the tunic's sleeves with Venetian glass beads interlaced with silk "rat tail" cording. Fortuny was noted for his antiquarian intentions and scholarly treatment of classical dress, yet in the end, he invented rather than replicated a Hellenic style.

Mariano Fortuny, Italian (born Spain 1871–1949). Evening ensemble, pale-blue pleated silk, 1934. The Metropolitan Museum of Art, The Costume Institute, Gift of Mrs. Anthony Wilson, 1979 (1979.344.11a, b)

Madeleine Vionnet is arguably the pre-eminent twentieth-century practitioner of the *flou*, or draped dressmaking. Her great innovations occurred through her investigations of the bias and of the very structure of cloth to contribute to the ultimate fit of a garment. This image by Irving Penn is from a suite of photographs he made after Diana Vreeland's exhibitions of the nineteen-tens, -twenties, and -thirties. Vionnet's handkerchief dress, of which this white crepe is an example, was made in several variations. Here, four double-layered squares have been rotated ninety degrees to form regular diamond shapes. The diamonds are seamed together vertically at center-front, back, and either side, leaving four sets of triangles that fall in perfect swallowtail folds. The top corners of the diamond shapes are paired and seamed to form the shoulder straps, while the opposite bottom corners form the handkerchief-pointed hem. Vionnet's rotation of the squares results in a transformation of the grain— the direction of the warp and weft of the cloth—into "true" bias, fabric at its most elastic.

The paradox of Norma Kamali's innovative work is that it has often been based on the imagery and techniques of the classical past. Her boutique is an architectural metaphor for her juxtaposition of past and present—eighteenth-century sculptures of the Four Seasons in classical dress positioned in a minimal, even brutalist, concrete space. From her earliest collections, Kamali has been interested in the sensuality of draped fabric. Diana Vreeland, the visionary fashion editor and Special Consultant to The Costume Institute, requested a series of goddess ensembles for the Museum from one of Kamali's earliest collections. Made of silk with the tapes and corded pulls of functional parachutes, the gowns sought by Vreeland combined dramatic wet-drapery effects with the sensibility of an Army-Navy store's back stock, making them ideal for a contemporary Nike. In the more recent examples shown here, the application of details like pleating and handkerchief-pointed drapery is not unexpected in eveningwear. Kamali's originality, however, is to ascribe those elements to active sportswear, as in her swimsuit, the piece on the right in the illustration.

Norma Kamali, American (born 1945). Left: Dress, 1974; right: Bathing suit, 1989–1990; both of white polyester jersey. Courtesy of Norma Kamali for OMO/Norma Kamali, Inc.

Wide variations occur in the representation of textiles in classical art. It is clear that differences in the draping characteristics of a fabric's weight or material—wool or linen and more rarely cotton or silk—resulted in certain conventions of rendering. The ancient votive relief shown here depicts Demeter, in a woolen peplos with wide flutes in her skirt, presenting ears of wheat to Triptolemos. Persephone, in a linen chiton with tightly crimped folds, crowns Triptolemos with a wreath. In the layered juxtaposition of a himation, peplos, and chiton, the flatter surfaces of the woolen mantle and peplos suggest that the compressed folds of the linen chiton are a depiction of pleating rather than of drapery. Unlike the regularly spaced folds seen in Egyptian or Assyrian representations, the fine, somewhat irregular texture suggests that the pleating is the product of a tightly bound compression of the textile, a technique still seen in certain regional dress traditions. In contrast to wool, which has a spring-like elasticity, the fibers of linen are easily creased and pleated.

The Great Eleusinian Relief: Demeter, Triptolemos, and Persephone. Fragments of a Roman copy set in a plaster cast of the original Greek relief, ca. 27 B.C.–14 A.D. The Metropolitan Museum of Art, Rogers Fund, 1914 (14.130.9)

Mariano Fortuny's pleated gowns have come to be surrounded by myth. Since his death in 1949, their production has ceased, although many of his textile designs continue to be made. Highly secretive about the processes employed in all of his designs, Fortuny left only one document related to the development of his delphos and peplos gowns, a patent for heated ceramic rollers through which silk was apparently passed to set the pleats. The use of the rollers, however, was probably a final stage in the creation of the dresses. Photographs of his earliest delphos gowns reveal a wave-like regularity of the pleating, unlike the later irregular and disrupted creases that characterize his signature dresses. The late Elizabeth Lawrence, a costume conservator, believed that the panels of silk were stitched loosely by hand selvage to selvage, the width of the fabric, with a thick basting thread. When the stitcher reached the edge, the needle was reversed about three-quarters of an inch above the last line of stitches, and a new line was made. This process then continued back and forth in a zig-zag pattern, through the whole length of the fabric. At the end of the panel, the thread was pulled in tightly, creating a narrowly compressed twist of fabric. This stitched hank was then passed through the heated rollers. More recently, costume scholars have come to believe that the process was much simpler, and that the fabric was tied at short intervals after being bunched by hand, like a traditional technique used in tie-dyeing in many countries. In either instance, the process would not set the pleats permanently. Clients had to send their dresses back to the Fortuny workshops to have the pleats reset if they were inadvertently dampened or flattened out at the seat.

Mariano Fortuny, Italian (born Spain 1871–1949). Evening gown, hand-dyed pleated silk, 1923. Photograph by James Abbe (1883–1973) of Natasha Rambova, wife of Rudolph Valentino, courtesy of James Abbe 1923 © Kathryn Abbe

Mary McFadden's pleated dresses begin with a fine satin-backed cloth developed and obtained in Australia. The synthetic, almost translucent fabric undergoes a number of carefully controlled processes, which include its dyeing in Japan and its pleating in the United States. The latter patented process involves over three separate steps and is called "Marii" pleating, after the designer. The resulting pleats have an organic irregularity that, with the light weight of the fabric, creates a supple body-skimming fit. Despite their appearance of fragility, McFadden's evening gowns are virtually indestructible, because of the polyester fiber that is the basis of the cloth. Unlike Fortuny's gowns, her dresses permanently hold their pleats. McFadden's designs convey her deep interest in distant cultures and times. In contrast to many of her colleagues, who plunder other periods for their forms with only a cursory understanding of their meanings, McFadden reflects in her designs an archaeologist's fascination with the cultures and narratives expressed through art. She is knowledgeable in a wide range of the esoteric and the exotic, and her designs, while indebted to the aesthetic of the classical antique, are informed by a sybaritic exoticism. The result is that her goddess dresses often carry an additional orientalist aura of Empress Theodora and the Byzantine court.

Mary McFadden, American (born 1938). Two evening gowns, ivory pleated synthetic fabric, fall–winter 1991. Courtesy of Mary McFadden

MYTHIC DETAILS: THE GREEK KEY, LAURELS,
AND THE ATTRIBUTES OF GODDESSES

Most early post-classical depictions of ancient Grecian themes represent the gods, demi-gods, and mortals in loosely draped, monochromatic robes. If present at all, the only ornamentation is a narrow banded border of braid or embroidery. However, pottery, painted sculptures, and the written word have given us extensive evidence of the use of decorative embellishments in ancient Greek dress. A cursory survey of red-and-black figure vase paintings alone reveals that antique dress was composed of a rich variety of graphically patterned textiles.

Among the most common designs seen in ancient art is the Greek-key pattern, a rectilinear meander. Other abstracted forms of wave patterns, geometric repeats, and palmette friezes are also seen on classical garments, as are more intricate borders depicting themes ranging from animals, birds, and fish to complex battle scenes. Nevertheless, such patterns have rarely been used by later artists or by contemporary designers. Of all these motifs, the Greek key and wave meander appear most frequently in designs intended to invoke the antique. In some instances, the key pattern is broken into a discontinuous segmented band, but even this disrupted linear repeat is sufficient to sustain the classical connection.

Although well represented in art, the use of mythological attributes to designate an Olympian deity is less common in fashion. However, the ancient Greek practice of recognizing achievement and bestowing honor through the presentation of a coronet of flowers and leaves has been adumbrated in neoclassical period embroideries and in the more recent work of a number of designers. The materials comprising the coronets originally associated with the presiding deities—laurels for Apollo, olive leaves for Athena, roses for Aphrodite, ivy for Dionysos—were perhaps too esoteric for the purposes of fashion and have generally been obscured. But other mythic attributes have continued with their original meanings intact. Designers as disparate in style as Christian Dior, Valentino, Alexander McQueen, and Gianni Versace have incorporated in their work attributes symbolic of Greek goddesses—peacock feathers for Hera, the aegis, or breastplate, for Athena, or sea foam and shells for Aphrodite.

Over time, reductive simplicity emerged as a way of conveying an aura of the antique, a strategy that was further developed in the nineteenth and twentieth centuries. But the classical past has also been evoked in dress by the application of patterns and designs from the repertoire of ancient ornament, as well as by referencing the various attributes of the Olympian deities. Incorporating these elements into their creations, contemporary designers have introduced to fashion the narratives of ancient myth. In a field characterized by constant change, they have clung to the illusion of an enduring and persistent ideal of beauty through the resonant imagery of classical decorative motifs.

The figures in this vase painting are thought to be preparing for a civic festival in celebration of the dead. Because they are in the act of perfuming garments for the event, the delineation of the garment pieces is particularly detailed. A woman in a finely pleated chiton and band-bordered himation on the right gestures toward another woman accompanied by a child. Bent over to pour fragrance into a bundle of cloth, the woman on the left wears a linen chiton and a short overtunic, not unlike the astrochiton associated with Artemis. While the astrochiton was covered with a pattern of stars, in this garment zones of pictographs alternate with Greek-key bands. A swing at center is stacked with neatly folded garments, with the border of the uppermost garment also patterned with the Greek key. Likewise, a klismos chair is piled with what appear to be a pleated chiton and another astrochiton with pictographs, Greek-key borders and an edge of palmette motifs. The ubiquity of the Greek key in textile patterns is also evidenced in the headscarves of both women.

Greek (Attic). *Oinochoe: Women Perfuming Clothes*, red figure vase, ca. 420–410 B.C. The Metropolitan Museum of Art, Gift of Samuel G. Ward, 1875 (75.2.11)

The use of decorative motifs associated with the Græco-Roman antique is one of the strategies employed by artists of later periods to situate the narratives of their work in the classical world. Of all the patterns that appear as woven, printed, or embroidered details in later textiles and dress, the Greek key, or rectilinear meander, is the most familiarly cited to establish the classicism of the design. In this fashion plate, from the decade immediately following the Empire period, the columnar silhouette, raised waistline, and small narrow sleeves that were intended to evoke classical dress have given way to more buoyant forms. The only neoclassical vestige is in the use of a foliate meander on the ribbon belting and of the Greek key as an embroidered band across the skirt.

French. "Petit Courrier des Dames," illustrated in *Modes de Paris*, 1826. The Metropolitan Museum of Art, The Irene Lewisohn Costume Reference Library, Woodman-Thompson Collection

The 1860s and 1870s saw the revival of a number of historical periods in dress. Oddly, the late-eighteenth-century bouffant skirts identified with the French pre-revolutionary aristocrats, were merged with the Grecian Bend, an effect from the post-revolutionary neoclassical period. The latter was a postural change, a hunched back, thought to be evocative of the faintly rounded stoop seen in such classical examples as the *Capitoline Venus* and the *Venus de'Medici*. In addition to such modifications of the high fashion silhouette, classical references were apparent in the appearance of laurel swags, wave meanders, and Greek-key bands on such categories of apparel as children's dresses, men's smoking ensembles, and dressing gowns, and on all forms of womenswear and accessories. In the bathing costume shown here, the connection to the natural and healthful life of "sport" associated with the ancient Greeks is especially apt. Of course, the wool cloth, heavy and hardly buoyant when wet, was not appropriate for vigorous water sports. Rather it was meant for what was considered the more feminine activity of "bathing," a simple immersion that allowed for some bobbing or a few strokes without any real possibility of sustained swimming.

American. Bathing ensemble, beige-and-brown printed striped wool with brown-and-red printed wool bands with Greek-key motif, ca. 1870.

The Metropolitan Museum of Art, The Costume Institute, Gift of the New York Historical Society, 1979 (1979.346.18a, b)

The allusions to classicism that infused the decade of the 1930s were often indirect. However, the Græco-Roman references in the fashions of the famous MGM movie costume designer Gilbert Adrian were generally more explicit, taking the form of Greek-key and wave meander embroideries superimposed on his signature fluidly draped silhouettes. Adrian's classical interests also appeared in his atelier in Beverly Hills, his boutiques in specialty stores, and his advertisements, which he art directed with interior designer and jeweler Tony Duquette. All were ornamented with suavely attenuated Ionic columns. He also underscored the classical references of his Hollywood goddess gowns by giving them names like "Statuesque" and "Patrician." Although, in both films and real life, he designed the wardrobes of many of the great actresses of Hollywood's heyday—Greta Garbo, Katherine Hepburn, Jean Harlow, Norma Shearer, and Joan Crawford—Adrian did not generally dress Marlene Dietrich, who was not contracted to MGM. That she would be photographed in one of his gowns suggests the universal appeal of his simple but boldly graphic glamour—not to mention the canniness of the actress to align herself with the enduring iconography of classical beauty.

Gilbert Adrian, American (1903–1959). Evening gown, ivory silk chiffon embroidered with beads and rhinestones, 1946. Photograph of Marlene Dietrich courtesy of Photofest

Designer Gianni Versace was known for the theatrical and hedonistic exuberance of his work. Both his tailoring and his dressmaking were characterized by body-contouring cuts and no small amount of exposure. The dramatic, in-the-kleig-lights glamour of his designs made him a favorite of movie stars and rock musicians. The Versace house logo, a Medusa-head medallion, is only one manifestation of his Græco-Roman influence. Versace's work was less informed by antiquity than the more extravagant Napoleonic manifestations of neoclassicism as it was filtered through the lens of the 1950s Roman film studio Cinecitta's Technicolor mythology. His celebration of uninhibited extroversion is seen in this short motorcycle jacket. The black leather and silver metallic studding introduce the dangerous attractions of social marginality associated with Hell's Angels and sexual fetishism. A Greek-key pattern enlivens both jacket and matching mini-kilt. Accessorized with cap, chain belts, and boots, Versace's ensemble constructs the persona of a contemporary gladiatrix, part biker moll and part rock goddess.

Gianni Versace, Italian (1946–1997). Ensemble, studded black leather, fall–winter 1992. Photograph: Sante d'Orazio

Reviving a technique used in the 1920s for metal mesh bags, Douglas Ferguson's late-twentieth century silhouettes overlay classical references on a medieval chainmail-like material. Like other conflations of recognizable period styles, his designs have the paradoxical effect of being outside time. It is a strategy used by costume designers in theater and the cinema, by illustrators in comic books, and more recently, by creators of computer games, to suggest utopias and dystopias, the future and imaginary parallel realities. Although the mesh is from Whiting and Davis, the original manufacturer of the bags, Ferguson has devised his own techniques for patterning their surface, exploiting the durability of enamel paints used for cars to create his coruscating designs. Although the mesh is kept in relatively unaltered rectilinear panels, individual components of the material, quatrefoil links, may be removed to modify the shape of each pattern piece. The minimal intervention required by the material, which flows over the body's contours, results in a structural simplicity similar to that of the uncut draped garments of the Greeks.

Douglas Ferguson, American (born 1951). Three evening ensembles, white, black, silver and gold enameled metal mesh with Greek-key motif, 1985.

Courtesy of Douglas Ferguson, NYC

In Greek mythology, maenads, or Bacchantes, are women votaries of Dionysos, the god of wine. Waving the thyrsos, a staff of fennel stalk with ivy and ivy berries as they sang, they abandoned themselves to orgiastic dancing and festivity. In the relief shown on the previous pages, the maenad wears a wreath of ivy leaves. The practice of wearing garlands in celebration of a deity is best known through the tradition of bestowing a wreath of laurels to honor achievement. The components of the garland identified not only the honor but also the presiding god or goddess. For designers, the many examples of hammered-gold coronets found in tombs and the extensive foliate bands on artworks established the leaf pattern as a classicizing motif.

The adaptation of this imagery is exemplified by the waist cinches on the two deceptively simple gowns by Madeleine Vionnet shown to the right. Vionnet introduced the body-skimming fit of her garments by exploiting the elastic qualities of the bias. Above all, Vionnet prized economy of cut and desired an idealized geometry in her pattern pieces. In her definitive monograph on Vionnet's oeuvre, Betty Kirke described much of the designer's work by the shapes of her pattern pieces: rectangles, circles, and quadrants. Despite the minimalist construction of her designs, Vionnet did not abhor the decorative. The belts required for the shaping of the two gowns shown here are enhanced by their aura of the antique. The overlapping gilded leather leaves evoke the foliate motifs of laurel, ivy, and olive-leaf wreaths, and are an intentional reference to the antique. Vionnet announced her affinity to the classical past by lining her couture salon with murals in Hellenistic style. Her logo of a woman standing on an Ionic capital appeared in her advertisements and on her label, further underscoring her classical affinities.

Previous pages: Roman copy of Greek original. *Dancing Maenad* (detail), marble relief, ca. 27 B.C.–14 A.D. The Metropolitan Museum of Art, Fletcher Fund, 1935 (35.11.3). Photograph: Scott Houston. Right: Madeleine Vionnet, French (1876–1975). Two evening gowns, silk with leather belt, 1936. Retouched photograph by George Hoyningen-Huene, Russian (1900–1968) courtesy of *Harper's Bazaar*

Mary McFadden's collections have been inspired by ancient cultures, exotic techniques, and mystical narratives. Her synthetic vision and her archaeological methodology have resulted in convincing fictions. The shaping of this spare slip dress originates from a series of released pintucks, a technique originally associated with lingerie. Although it projects the simplicity of a nymph's chiton, the major suggestion of the classical is not the silhouette or the soft travertine ivory of the silk. Nor is it the tucking that, like the pleated flutes of her signature gowns, recalls the columnar forms of neoclassical styles. Instead, it is the brass foliage resembling the hammered-gold laurels found in ancient Greek tombs that sprout on the vine-like tendrils binding the shoulders. The soft upholstered cords knotted at their ends, to which the leaves are anchored, are a McFadden signature. They appear to derive from the tubular cotton-stuffed cords used by the Japanese to secure the obi, the wide decorative sash worn with a kimono. This transposition of a costume detail from one context into another is a typically fantastical and arresting McFadden conflation.

Mary McFadden, American (born 1938). Dress, ivory pin-tucked silk satin, ca. 1976. Lent by The Museum at The Fashion Institute of Technology, Gift of Naomi Sims (81.145.4)

Minerva, Athena to the Greeks, wears a peplos with a single waist tie. Because the gown has not been undergirdled into a kolpos, an especially wide peplum is formed by the extra-deep apoptygma. Among Athena's attributes, especially in her role as warrior and protectoress of Athens, was the aegis, or pectoral, a protective piece originally of leather that shielded the neck and chest from blows. Athena's aegis was often depicted as a skin bordered by serpents and emblazoned with the head of Medusa, a Gorgon. Over time, the idea of the aegis was incorporated into contemporary armorial styles, with the goddess in the seventeenth-century, for example, wearing a ceremonial breastplate appropriate to that era but emblazoned with the Medusa. The association of the handsome virgin goddess with the petrifying countenance of the serpent-tressed monster has suggested a provocative iconography of martial feminist power to some contemporary designers.

Minerva with the Pectoral, marble, Roman adaptation of a Greek original of the 5th century B.C. Paris, Musée du Louvre. Photograph © Réunion des Musées Nationaux/Art Resource, NY

Paul Nadar's photograph of the Marquise d'Hervey de Saint-Denis documents her costume as Minerva, Athena to the Greeks, for a fancy dress ball given by the Princess de Sagan. The Marquise, a model for Marcel Proust's Princess d'Orvillers, conjures the Græco-Roman goddess through the aesthetics of late-seventeenth- and early-eighteenth century French fashion. Her asymmetrical skirt, cut like an open robe with its petticoat gathered up at her right hem, and voluminous train allude to the draperies of antiquity. But it is with her breastplate, ostrich-plumed headdress, and owl-topped staff that the iconography becomes more explicitly associated with Minerva. Unlike the pectoral aegis generally shown on the goddess in ancient Hellenic examples, the Marquise is armored in a breastplate that is half ceremonial cuirasse and half corselet. The Medusa head that embellishes the breastplate is rendered with the monster's serpentine tresses as a radiating coronet. Like the other elements of her costume, this original attribute has been re-imagined with a picturesque splendor. As with this example of fancy dress, recent fashion has assimilated some of the iconography of classical goddesses. In the case of Minerva, the breastplate functions as the most persistently resonant of her attributes.

Paul Nadar, French (1856–1939). *The Marquise d'Hervey de Saint-Denis as Minerva*, photograph, 1892. Photograph: Paul Nadar, Archives © CMN, Paris

Alexander McQueen's first collection as designer for Givenchy Haute Couture was held in the ornate confines of the Ecole des Beaux-Arts, the art academy founded in 1648 that was for centuries the primary conduit for the dissemination of classical style. Surrounded by gilt and marble, men with minimally, if carefully draped loins were perched on Doric columns, serving as frames for the presentation. Like Eros, they were armed with bows, establishing the mood of the collection—the antique seen through the eyes of Jean Berain, the prolific designer of decorative arts, costumes, and theatrical sets in the Court of Louis XIV. The gorget is an armorial element intended to protect the throat of the wearer from the glance of a sword. This gilded version was originally part of a McQueen ensemble of chimerical mix—a white suit with a python skin coat, sheepskin and ram's horned hat, and a nose ring of the type to subdue bulls. In this photograph, Eric Traoré transformed the piece by removing it from its original context and pairing it with gilt ear ornaments from another design in the collection. Although the original ensemble would not be out of place in one of Ovid's stories, the gorget in isolation suggests a conventional attribute of Athena, the wearing of an aegis. Here, the pattern of feathers has nothing to do with the snake-fringed Gorgon-head embellished armor typically associated with the goddess, but it does evoke her sacred bird, the owl. Warrior women appear as a leitmotif in McQueen's work. He has said that his clothing is intended to "confer an air of invincibility" to women. The photographer's re-situation of the piece appropriates a new meaning, unintended by the designer but consistent with his belief in the power of women: the martial authority of Athena.

Givenchy Haute Couture, French (founded 1952), by Alexander McQueen, British (born 1969). Gold feather gorget and gold ear ornaments, spring–summer 1997. Photograph: Eric Traoré

Oscar de la Renta's ready-to-wear collections have always conveyed an haute couture aura. As the designer for Balmain, he infused a fresh American pragmatism into the ethereal world of haute couture, which has recently been characterized by a trend toward mediagenic "only for the runway" fantasy. In either milieu, however, de la Renta is known for designs of elegant and often sumptuous luxury, perfectly suited to the lives of his sophisticated clients. His exploration of the couture atelier's extraordinary artisanal possibilities has yielded evening designs of subtle refinements not possible in the ready-to-wear. For example, in this ensemble from his final collection at Balmain, de la Renta referenced Minerva, the goddess of wisdom. Perhaps alluding to her favorite bird, the owl, de la Renta created a breastplate of gilt cock feathers that have been hand-clipped and overlapped in carefully graduated rows. For all its illusion of metallic heft, the breastplate is literally featherweight; each pinion has been individually attached to a silk net ground that is lined in silk organza. Paired with a long skirt of crimped-and-pleated gold gauze, the ensemble suggests a contemporary feminine counterpart to Louis XIV's well-known costume in which he portrayed Apollo. In seventeenth-century fancy dress, and in twenty-first-century evening dress, the breastplate is both an attribute associated with a deity and an opportunity for brilliantly gilded display.

Pierre Balmain Haute Couture, French (founded 1945), by Oscar de la Renta, American (born Santo Domingo 1932). "Minerva" evening ensemble, metallic gold-painted feathers and pleated gold lamé, fall–winter 2002. Courtesy of Pierre Balmain Haute Couture

Here, Alexander McQueen's interpretation of classical armor is used by the photographers Pierre & Gilles to costume the celebrated model Naomi Campbell as Diana, Artemis to the Greeks. McQueen took the molded breastplate that originally would have been of metal and the tabulated leather overskirt worn by Greek warriors over their short chitons, and merged them into one garment. In the designer's rendering, the leather is gilded, befitting a classical deity or the resplendent, often archaized ceremonial armors of later date. The appropriation of male martial attire to the female form conforms better to the iconography of Minerva, Athena to the Greeks, the warrior goddess, than to Diana, the huntress. But the identification of the ensemble with either deity would appeal to McQueen; both are virginal but endowed with a physical prowess normally restricted to men. In this example, two of the designer's favorite themes converge—feminine power and the classical past.

Givenchy Haute Couture, French (founded 1952), by Alexander McQueen, British (born 1969). Evening dress, gold leather, fall–winter 1997.

Naomi Campbell as Diana © Pierre & Gilles. Photograph courtesy of Galerie Jérôme de Noirmont, Paris

As seen on the preceding two pages, Italian Renaissance master Sandro Botticelli's *Birth of Venus* depicts the goddess of beauty on a seashell, carried by waves to the shores of Cythera. Because the subject of the painting predicates the nudity of the goddess, the painter compensated for the absence of apparel by giving his Venus, the Greek Aphrodite, a long twist of thick hair. These tresses function as a device for modesty, just as the coiled himation does in classical sculpture. Through images such as this, Venus, born of the sea, came to be represented by glittering embroideries intended to replicate foaming waves. Unlike their depictions of Athena, Renaissance artists had to rely on literary references for knowledge of the attributes of Aphrodite, since in surviving antique artworks, she is generally depicted nude or half-dressed. Contemporary designers have looked to these sixteenth-century representations and later permutations and incorporated the imagery into their work. For example, the extraordinary ball gown by Christian Dior shown to the left, of foggy gray silk tulle, arrayed with an overlay of scallop-shaped petals, is called "Venus." The bodice and shell forms of its skirt are embellished with nacreous paillettes and sequins, iridescent seed beads, aurora-borealis crystals, and pearls. The glittering overskirt and train adumbrate both the seashell motif and the crescent wave patterns of Botticelli's Venus. Dior is best known for his revival of the wasp-waisted silhouette seen here. His celebrated first collection of 1947 was dubbed the "New Look" by the influential American editor Carmel Snow, because the corseted, full-bosomed, and hourglass shaping had not been seen for decades. In fact, the "New Look" was an old look revived. After the deprivations of World War II, Dior believed that the survival of the haute couture relied on its ability to restore fantasy and luxury to women's wardrobes. The fragile effects of this gown, which merges Second-Empire romanticism with the classical iconography of ideal and eternal beauty, recall Dior's belief that "fashion comes from a dream."

Preceding pages: Sandro Botticelli, Italian (1444–1510). *Birth of Venus*, tempera on canvas, ca. 1485. Firenze, Galleria degli Uffizi/Art Resource. Left: Christian Dior, French (1905–1957). "Venus" dress, gray silk net embroidered with feather-shaped opalescent sequins, rhinestones, simulated pearls, and paillettes, 1949. The Metropolitan Museum of Art, The Costume Institute, Gift of Mrs. Byron C. Foy, 1953 (CI 53.40.7a-e)

Gianni Versace's love of classical themes is evident in the Medusa-head logo that established his atelier's identity. The Versace goddess is worldly, without the idealized aura of the Hellenic arcadia. Her confidence is almost brazen, and her taste for spectacular effects is uninhibited. In Versace's imagination, classical dress was an opportunity for body-revealing drape and incandescent effects. This gown's silver satin sheathes the torso, then opens up to fanning pleats at the skirt. Arcing inserts of silver gauze, with iridescent paillettes and crystal beads densely embroidered at their crest, waft over the wearer's legs in a wave-like undulation, opening the gown and exposing the body beneath. In repose, the satin pleats endow the wearer with a columnar dignity, but in motion, the disclosure of the body and the liquid drift of the sheer fabric suggest Venus emerging from the sea.

Gianni Versace, Italian (1946–1997). Evening gown, silver silk satin and silver synthetic lamé embroidered with clear and silver pailettes and beads, spring–summer 1996. The Metropolitan Museum of Art, The Costume Institute, Gift of Donatella Versace, 1999 (1999.328.4)

By 1949, Christian Dior's instinct for calibrated innovations of the body's "line" had established him as fashion's preeminent arbiter. That year, dresses called "Venus" and "Junon," or Hera to the Greeks, were among the most coveted of his designs. Dior's Venus was realized in the delicate eighteenth-century gray that was his signature, frosted with iridescent beading and embroidery. But his Junon, the design on the facing page, is more vividly conceived. The magnificent skirt of ombréed petals, like abstractions of peacock feathers without their "eyes," obliquely references the bird associated with the Queen of the Olympians. By contrast, Emanuel Ungaro's classical gown, shown on the overleaf at right, like the magnificent peplos and capacious himation befitting the noblest Olympian goddess, is discreet in its coverage. With the attributes of the Græco-Roman gods so clearly defined, it is possible to ascribe mythic identities to contemporary garments even in the absence of explicit identifications. The body-exposing drape of Tom Ford's gown on the overleaf at left is easily associated with Aphrodite, the goddess of beauty, and the short dress by Versace at center, with its neckline secured by a tape, would be ideal for the athletic Artemis. Current notions of classical dress are surprising in the breadth of their parameters. They are based in part on the original variations and manipulations of the antique models, the attributes accrued to it over time by artistic convention, and the twentieth-century adaptation of ancient methods to modern forms. That the dress of people two-and-a-half millennia in the past can imbue a design of today with the aura of myth and timeless beauty suggests that the classical mode, like Penelope's weaving, is continuous and without end.

Left: Christian Dior, French (1905–1957). "Junon" dress, pale-blue silk net embroidered with iridescent blue, green and rust sequins, 1949. The Metropolitan Museum of Art, The Costume Institute, Gift of Mrs. Byron C. Foy, 1953 (CI 53.40.5a-e). Overleaf left: Gucci, Italian (founded 1921) by Tom Ford, American (born 1961). Evening dress, pink silk jersey, spring–summer 2003. Courtesy of Gucci. Overleaf center: Gianni Versace, Italian (1946–1997). Evening dress, cream silk jersey, ca. 1983. Courtesy of Milan Tainan, Justsaywhen.com. Overleaf right: Emanuel Ungaro, French (born 1933). Evening ensemble, gray silk crepe and gray silk chiffon, ca. 1990–1992. The Metropolitan Museum of Art, The Costume Institute, Gift of Anne H. Bass, 1993 (1993.345.15a-c)

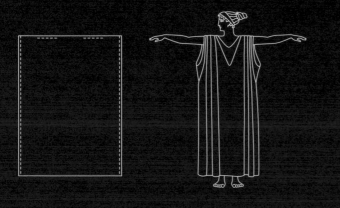

CHITON

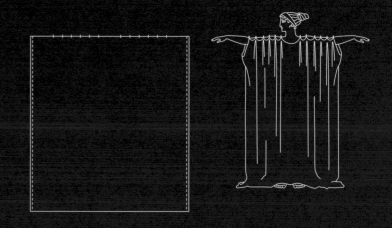

FULL CHITON

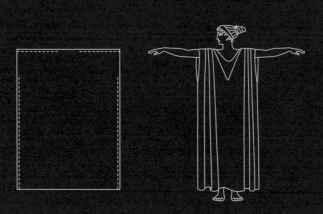

CHITON VARIATION

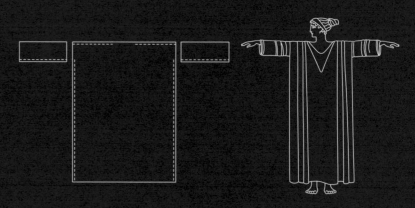

CHITON VARIATION WITH SLEEVES

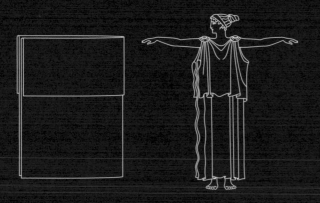

OPEN PEPLOS

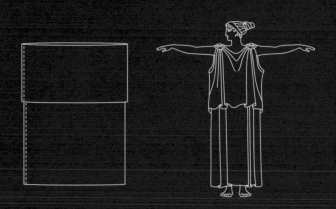

CLOSED PEPLOS

The terms describing ancient Greek dress in this publication are of a general character, and, for reasons explained in the Introduction, do not conform necessarily with definitions of scholars, specialists, and students of the field. They are accompanied on the facing page by drawings derived from the original work of Anastasia Pekridou-Gorecki. Although small adjustments have been introduced to her concise diagrams for the purposes of readability to a broad audience, the template of her research and studies is clear.

APOPTYGMA: The overfold at the top of a peplos.

CHITON: The chemise-like shift worn exclusively by men in a knee-length form and by men and women in a floor-length version. Constructed of two rectangles of fabric, generally of linen, the chiton was seamed together in a number of variations. One style was stitched like a closed poncho along the shoulderline and sideseams, with apertures left at the top edge and upper sideseams for the head and arms. A variation of this form incorporated two small rectangular sleeve pieces that made a T-shaped garment. However, the most characteristically Greek variation was accomplished by stitching the two rectangular pieces of fabric together along either sideseam, from top to bottom, forming a cylinder with its top edge and hem unstitched. The top edges were then sewn or pinned together to form shoulder seams. The resulting shoulderline orientation of the armhole, perpendicular to the sideseam, introduced a dolman-style drape to the underarm area of the garment. If the rectangles were cut very wide, the topline was pinned at short intervals, creating a fissured shoulderline sometimes referred to as the Ionic sleeve.

CHLAMYS: The short cloak, or mantle, worn by men.

HIMATION: The wide rectangular cloak, or mantle, worn by both men and women.

KOLPOS: The blouson formed by belting and girdling the chiton and peplos.

PEPLOS: Made of one large rectangular piece of cloth, the peplos was folded in half to form a cylinder, and then a second time along the topline in a deep cuff, forming an overfold, or apoptygma. The shoulders of the peplos were created by fibulae, brooch-like pins that attached the front to the back of the garment at either side. Like the most distinctively Greek form of the chiton, the orientation of the armhole of the peplos was along the topline of the cylinder, creating folds at either underarm area. The right side of the peplos was sometimes left unstitched but more commonly was sewn closed.

SELECTED BIBLIOGRAPHY

Boardman, J. *The Diffusion of Classical Art in Antiquity*. A.W. Mellon lectures in the fine arts, 1993. Bollingen Series XXXV, 42. London: Thames and Hudson, 1994.

Croom, A.T. *Roman Clothing and Fashion*. Stroud: Tempus, 2000.

Die griechische Klassik: Idee oder Wirklichkeit: eine Ausstellung im Martin-Gropius-Bau. Verlag Phillip van Zabern, 2002.

D'après L'antique: Paris, Musée du Louvre, 16 October 2000–15 January 2001. Paris: Réunion des Musées Nationaux, 2000.

Haskell, Francis, and Nicholas Penny. *Taste and the Antique: The Lure of Classical Sculpture, 1500–1900*. New Haven: Yale University Press, 1981.

Heuzey, Léon. *Histoire du Costume Antique*. Paris: Librairie Ancienne Honoré Champion, 1922.

Johnson, Marie. *Ancient Greek Dress: A New Illustrated Edition Combining Greek Dress by Ethel Abrahams [and] Chapters on Greek Dress by Lady Evans*. Chicago: Argonaut, 1964.

Llewellyn-Jones, Lloyd (ed.). *Women's Dress in the Ancient Greek World*. London: Duckworth: Swansea: Classical Press of Wales, 2002.

Losfeld, Georges. *Essai sur le Costume Grec*. Paris: Éditions de Boccard, 1991.

Morrow, Katherine Dohan. *Greek Footwear and the Dating of Sculpture*. Wisconsin Studies in Classics. Madison: University of Wisconsin Press, 1985.

Neils, Jenifer, et al. *Goddess and Polis: the Panathenaic Festival in Ancient Athens*. Hanover: Hood Museum of Art, Dartmouth College; Princeton: Princeton University Press, 1992.

Pekridou-Gorecki, Anastasia. *Mode im Antiken Griechenland: Textile Fertigung und Kleidung*. München: C.H. Beck, 1989.

Sebesta, Judith Lynn, and Larissa Bonfante (ed.). *The World of Roman Costume*. Madison: University of Wisconsin Press, 1994.

Acknowledgments

This book and the exhibition it accompanies would not have been possible were it not for the participation and generosity of a veritable pantheon of colleagues, associates and friends of The Costume Institute. Philippe de Montebello, Director of the Metropolitan Museum of Art, has supported the idea for "Goddess" from the beginning, and allowed me, as the gods do with mortals in all Greek myths, to reap the consequences of my own mischief. For "Goddess" our galleries would be an underworld of darkness and void without the support of Condé Nast and Gucci. Anna Wintour has been as with so many past projects our Pallas Athena, protective warrior goddess and advocate of our pursuit of new interpretations of dress. Our Apollo, Tom Ford, immediately steered the gilded Gucci chariot, known for its extensive philanthropy to the contemporary arts, in the direction of The Costume Institute and the Museum.

The contributions of The Costume Institute staff, fellows and interns have exceeded once again any reasonable expectation. Maya Naunton, Caitlin O'Grady, and Jessica Regan, directed by our conservator Chris Paulocik, are responsible for the gentle vivification of each object. Lisa Faibish, who has styled each mannequin, and Karin Willis, our photographer, are the Gemini collaboration that has yielded the cooly classical images of dresses from both The Costume Institute and the collections of lenders. Shannon Bell, Charles Hansen, and Joyce Fung have had to bear the main brunt of this Herculean organizational effort, although Valerie Boisseau-Tulloch, Beth Dincuff Charleston, Michael Downer, Stéphane Houy-Towner, Jessa Krick, Tatyana Pakhladzhyan, Laura Riley, Elyssa Schram, and Melinda Webber Kerstein have each been conscripted at different points to address the vexing problems and challenges released from this Pandora's Box of a project. Lita Semerad was my Ariadne, providing the administrative thread that lead me out of a labyrinth of commitments and deadlines. Our search for elusive loans was abetted by Rose Simon's invaluable network of associations. Although they are our three Graces, Cynthia Cunningham, Michele Chase, and Oriole Cullen pursued objects and research for the exhibition with the tenacity of Furies. Despina Giavridi Vasanelli shared many of the ideas in her graduate thesis and helped me out of the Hades of nomenclature, an unfamiliar world where everything was Greek. Andrew Bolton, like Hephaestos, helped to forge my amorphous thoughts into more useful shape.

The Museum's Editor in Chief, John P. O'Neill, has done everything to shepherd this project to a successful conclusion. In this he has been assisted capably and with notable patience by Gwen Roginsky, Associate General Manager of Publications, and Elisa Frohlich, Production Manager. The book's elegance and formal lucidity are due to Takaaki Matsumoto and his staff. Even a terrifying Hydra of deadlines did not perturb their professionalism and calm. Thanh X. Tran drew the sketches derived from the original work of Anastasia Pekridou-Gorecki that accompany the glossary and Amy Wilkins whose final review of all visual and textual materials submitted saved me from any number of pitfalls. Her conscientiousness and care were crucial to this effort. Barbara Cavaliere, our editor, was both astute and heroic in her extensive refinement of the rudiments of my text into its present form. As in our past projects together, I have relied on her insights and knowledge. Without her and her advocacy there would be no book.

The Metropolitan Museum of Art is comprehensive in its range of scholarship and experience. Especially in a project such as this, the contribution of colleagues is critical to its success. My hubris in tackling this subject was precipitated by my confidence in the support of my friends in the Department of Greek and Roman Art. Carlos Picón's enthusiasm for the project consolidated my belief in its validity. Michael Baran like Hermes conveyed all the details and research of Greek and Roman artworks with efficient and speedy dispatch. Elizabeth J. Milleker on numerous occasions was my patient tutor in the readings of the artworks. My time with her in the galleries was simply inspiring. Her time with me poring over the galleys was perhaps for her, less so. I am grateful for both. The Department of Photographs, as always, has understood the peculiarities of a Costume Institute effort. Maria Morris Hambourg, Malcolm Daniel, and Mia Fineman accommodated our inconvenient timing of requests with unfailing good humor. The linkage of costume to the decorative arts of the twentieth century is compelling, and the willingness of the Modern Art Department to expand on my ambitions is manifested in the wonderful suggestions made by J. Stewart Johnson and Jared Goss.

The Museum's support of curatorial efforts takes the form of individuals of extraordinary skills and collegiality. Valerie Troyansky adjusted the Molding Studio schedule to free sculptor Ronald Street's intimidating calendar of commitments so that he could create the classicized wigs for our mannequins. Other Departments of the Museum are consistently taxed by the idiosyncratic requirements of The Costume Institute, but are without exception generous, even indulgent, of our needs and deadlines—Design: Jeff Daly, Sophia Geronimus, Dan Kershaw, Zack Zanolli, Clint Coller, Rich Lichte; Communications: Harold Holzer, Elyse Topalian, Bernice Kwok-Gable, Diana Pitt; Operations: Linda Sylling, Patricia Gilkison; Buildings: Taylor Miller; Photograph Studio: Barbara Bridgers, Chad Beer, Mark Morosse; Photograph and Slide Library: Deanna Cross, Lucinda K. Ross; Registrar's Office: Nina Maruca, Lisa Cain.

The many photographers, models and archives that have availed us of their images with notable generosity have comprised the core of the editorial project. Without their support, the idea of classicism's vitality could not have been as convincingly argued—James Abbe: Kathryn Abbe Photographs; Art Resource/NY: Andrea Begel; Artists Rights Society: Laura Strauss; Richard Avedon: Norma Stevens, Jennifer Landwehr; Bibliothèque Nationale de France, Paris; Naomi Campbell: Premiere Model Management; Condé Nast: Charlie Scheips, Leigh Montville, Michael Stier, Ena Wojciechowski; Corbis: Alyssa Sachar; Sante D'Orazio Studio Inc.: Diane Prete; Michele Filomeno Agency: Stéphane Allart; Adina Fohlin: Next Model Management/NY, Alexis Borges; Nathaniel Goldberg: The Katy Barker Agency, London, Catherine O'Brien; Bridget Hall: IMG, N. Jennings; Hiro Studio: Pieta Carnevale; Steven Klein Studios: Mark Mayer; Estate of George Platt Lynes: George P. Lynes, II, Executor; Maryland Historical Society, Baltimore: Ruth Mitchell; Steven Meisel: Art and Commerce, Jennifer Palmer; Julianne Moore: PMK/HBH, Stephen Huvane, Erica Gray; Museo Nacional del Prado: Concepción Ocampos; Paul Nadar Archives: Agence Photographique du Centre des Monuments Nationaux, Nathalie; Helmut Newton; Bost-Ienn: Isabelle Pantanacce; National Gallery of Art, Washington, D.C., Chester Dale Collection; New York Public Library Photographic Services, Tom Lisanti, Andrea Felder; L'Officiel: Office of Cecile Sepuchre; Irving Penn Studio Inc.: Dee Vitale Henle; Phoenix Art Museum: Leesha M. Alston; Photofest/NY: Ronald Mandelbaum; Pierre et Gilles: Jérôme de Noirmont, Galerie Jérôme de Noirmont, Paris; Prada: Anita Joos; Man Ray Archives: Telimage, Pierre-Yves Butzbach; Réunion des Musées Nationaux, Paris; Bert Stern: Bert Stern Photographs; Michael Thompson, Inc.: Shannon L. Urbon; Eric Traoré: Thomas and Carol Treuhaft; Christy Turlington: United Talent Agency, Lisa Jacobson; Maria C. Valentino: MCV Photo, Josephine Solimene; Amber Valletta: DNA Model Management, Didier Fernandez; Javier Vallhonrat: Nigel Boekee; Inez van Lamsweerde & Vinoodh Matadin: Jasper Bode; Vogue/British: Romney Park, Suzy Koo; Vogue/Paris: Stephanie Ovide Guarneri; Vogue/Deutsch: Christina Schubeck; Vogue/Nippon: Aya Fukamachi; Vogue/Italia: Paola Renna; Tsutomu Wakatsuki: Miyake Design Studio, Masako Omari; Yumiko Yata: Studio Voice Magazine, Japan; Getty Images: Valérie Zarś.

The opening of collections and the sharing of knowledge and artworks from a number of institutions in New York and elsewhere have been invaluable to a comprehensive realization of the subject—Bryn Mawr College: Alice Donohue; The Museum at The Fashion Institute of Technology: Valerie Steele, Fred Dennis, Anahid Akasheh, Glenn Petersen, Carmen Saavedra, Deborah Norden, Irving Solero; The Museum of the City of New York: Phyllis Magidson; New York Public Library for the Performing Arts, Jerome Robbins Dance Division, Madeleine M. Nichols, Grace Owen; The Fashion Institute of Design and Merchandising: Robert Nelson; The Kyoto Costume Institute: Yoshinori Satou, Akiko Takahashi Fukai, Makoto Ishizeki, Junichi Sakamoto; Los Angeles

County Museum of Art: Sharon Takeda, Kaye Spilker, Mary Levkoff; Musée Yves Saint Laurent: Hector Pascual, Romain Verdure; Museum of London: Edwina Ehrman, Antonia Charlton, Oriole Cullen; The Philadelphia Museum of Art: Dilys Blum.

The neo-classical gowns in The Costume Institute's collection have been augmented by wonderful examples from the following private collectors—Kelly Bensimon; Laird Borrelli; Hamish Bowles; Lauren Bush; Mrs. Randolph Hearst: Deborah Distasi; Alicia Keys: Terry Augello, Patty Wilson; Nicole Kidman: Shari Landon, Toby Fleischman; Jennifer Lopez: Benny Medina; Mary McFadden; Caroline Rennolds Milbank; Chris Royer; Rosina Rucci; Sandy Schreier; Cally Stavropoulos: Yveta Synek Graff; Mark Walsh. Many of them are old friends and supporters of our past efforts, but a notable few are important new relationships. Their marvelous loans have introduced a richness and depth to the core of our own holdings.

In the end, however, it is the creativity of designers that is the basis for our interests and investigations. The recent surprising and inventive interpretations of the dress of classical myth have connected us to the beauty of ancient Greece. In many instances, the extraordinary designs have been donated to us, situating this work in the rich history of fashion and enhancing the encyclopedic holdings of the Museum. I extend to these designers special thanks—Giorgio Armani: Jenna Barnet, Paula Decato; Balenciaga: Pureza Fino; Pierre Balmain Haute Couture: Katia Smirnoff, Camille Turpin Baumer; Oscar de la Renta: Boaz Mazor, Lisa Treiber; Bill Blass, Ltd.: Lars Nilsson, Michael Groveman, Yvonne Miller, Karen deFalco; Callaghan: Zamasport S.p.A., Maxence Dinant; Roberto Cavalli: Christiano Mancelli; Chado Ralph Rucci: Vivian VanNutta; Hussein Chalayan: Milly Patrzalek; Chanel Conservatoire: Marika Genty; Clements Ribeiro: Suzanne Clements, Inacio Ribeiro, BCPR/Beverly Cable PR, Teresa Ramsden; Christian Dior Couture: Bernard Danillon de Cazella, Soizic Pfaff; Dolce & Gabbana: Stephanie Turnier-Mori, Sarah Brooch; Donna Karan New York: Aliza Licht; Jacques Fath, Paris: Lizzie Disney, Christophe Verot; Fendi: Carla Gabetti, Angela Paoli; Douglas Ferguson; Alberta Ferretti: Christina Di Mauro Kelly, AEFFE USA Inc.; Shelley Fox Studio: Shelley Fox; John Galliano: Jelka Music; Romeo Gigli: Frans Ankoné; Givenchy: Mylène Lajoix; Gucci: Lisa Schiek, Arabella Rufino, Jennifer Pinto, Megan Stack; Carolina Herrera: Carolina Herrera, Jr., Anthony Lobasso; Tommy Hilfiger: Jo-Di Moore; Justsaywhen.com: Milan Tainan; Lainey Keough: Ellie Boyle; Christian Lacroix: Elizabeth Bonnel; La Perla: Naimeh Saatchi; Ralph Lauren: Bette-Ann Gwathmey, Rebecca Hirsch, Nicole Felsen; Fred Leighton Ltd.: Fred Leighton; m.r.s.: Molly Stern, Brett Erickson; Alexander McQueen: Kerry Youmans, Megan Woods; Issey Miyake: Jun Kanai, Masako Omari, Nancy Knox; Thierry Mugler: Renato Cavero; OMO Norma Kamali: Joanna Plisko; Rick Owens; Cesare Paciotti: Gaelle Dessauvages; Prada: Miuccia Prada, Jennifer Dornfeld; Arnold Scaasi: Scaasi Inc., Jerry Sirchia; Scherrer Haute Couture: Stéphane Rolland, Phillipe Angelotti, Christophe Verot; Toledo Studio: Isabel Toledo, Ruben Toledo, Andrea Eunterberger; Emanuel Ungaro: Sydney Goldman; Valentino Garavani: Valentino S.p.A., Carlos Souza; Gianni Versace: Patrizia Cuelco, Billy Daley; Vera Wang: Rebecca Fitts; Yohji Yamamoto: Carla Wachtveitl; YSL–Rive Gauche: Charlotte Rechtschaffen, Whitney DeLear.

"Goddess" has been a challenging but thrilling exploration for me. Unlike the capricious deities that impeded, even frustrated, the ambitions of the characters of Greek myth, I was only abetted by the encouragement and support of these uniformly generous people. Like the Olympian gods, however, they did have the ability transform my intangible thoughts into the reality of this book and exhibition.

Harold Koda
Curator in Charge, The Costume Institute
The Metropolitan Museum of Art